Welcome to the EVERYTHING® series!

THESE HANDY, accessible books give you all you need to tackle a difficult project, gain a new hobby, comprehend a fascinating topic, prepare for an exam, or even brush up on something you learned back in school but have since forgotten.

You can read an *EVERYTHING®* book from cover to cover or just pick out the information you want from our four useful boxes: e-facts, e-ssentials, e-alerts, and e-questions. We literally give you everything you need to know on the subject, but throw in a lot of fun stuff along the way, too.

We now have well over 100 *EVERYTHING®* books in print, spanning such wide-ranging topics as weddings, pregnancy, wine, learning guitar, one-pot cooking, managing people, and so much more. When you're done reading them all, you can finally say you know *EVERYTHING®*!

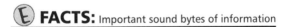

Ⓔ FACTS: Important sound bytes of information

Ⓔ ESSENTIALS: Quick and handy tips

Ⓔ ALERTS: Urgent warnings

Ⓔ QUESTIONS: Solutions to common problems

THE

EVERYTHING

Series

Dear Reader,

What does the word *bachelorette* mean to you? Does it conjure up an image of a wild Bacchanalian night complete with half-clothed men and a never-ending spring of champagne? Or is a quiet weekend of catching up with the girls and sipping hot buttered rum in a ski lodge more your style?

The wonderful thing about bachelorette parties is that you can tailor them to suit the bride's wishes, whatever they may be. The only limit is your imagination. The more freedom you allow yourself, the more creative and unique your party will be. Your only worry will be that all your friends will want you to organize their bachelorette parties!

We've planned lots of bachelorette parties and attended more than we can count. We've seen good ones and bad ones, out-of-hand bashes and subdued affairs. We've been to bachelorette parties with 100 guests, and those with fewer than ten. For every bride's taste, and for every hostess's pocketbook, there's a perfect bachelorette party just waiting to happen. Breathe easy, and put your faith in this book.

Jennifer Latin Ring   Shelly Hagen

THE
EVERYTHING
BACHELORETTE PARTY BOOK

Throw a party that the
bride—and her friends—
will never forget!

Jennifer Lata Rung &
Shelly Hagen

Adams Media Corporation
Avon, Massachusetts

An Everything® Series Book.
Everything® and everything.com® are registered trademarks of
Adams Media Corporation.

Published by Adams Media Corporation
57 Littlefield Street, Avon, MA 02322 U.S.A.
www.adamsmedia.com

ISBN: 1-58062-964-4
Printed in Canada.

J I H G F E D C B A

Library of Congress Cataloging-in-Publication Data
Rung, Jennifer Lata
The everything bachelorette party book /
Jennifer Lata Rung & Shelly Hagen.
p.   cm.
ISBN 1-58062-964-4
1. Bachelorette parties. I. Hagen, Shelly. II. Title.
GV1462.7.B33R86 2003
793.2—dc21
2003011088

This publication is designed to provide accurate and authoritative information with regard to the subject matter covered. It is sold with the understanding that the publisher is not engaged in rendering legal, accounting,
or other professional advice. If legal advice or other expert assistance is
required, the services of a competent professional person should be sought.
—From a *Declaration of Principles* jointly adopted by a
Committee of the American Bar Association and
a Committee of Publishers and Associations

Illustrations by Barry Littmann.

This book is available at quantity discounts for bulk purchases.
For information, call 1-800-872-5627.

THE

EVERYTHING
Series

EDITORIAL

Publishing Director: Gary M. Krebs
Managing Editor: Kate McBride
Copy Chief: Laura MacLaughlin
Acquisitions Editor: Bethany Brown
Development Editor: Julie Gutin
Production Editor: Khrysti Nazzaro

PRODUCTION

Production Director: Susan Beale
Production Manager: Michelle Roy Kelly
Series Designer: Daria Perreault
Cover Design: Paul Beatrice and Frank Rivera
Layout and Graphics: Colleen Cunningham,
Rachael Eiben, Michelle Roy Kelly,
Daria Perreault, Erin Ring

Visit the entire Everything® series at everything.com

Contents

Acknowledgments

Thanks to Jen Rung and Karyn Ulrich for being generous with their time and honest in their criticism, and to Jen (again) and my agent, Jessica Faust, for giving (and getting) me a chance.

—*Shelly Hagen*

Top Ten Reasons
to Host a Bachelorette Party

1. "Party" is your middle name.

2. You want to *really* get to know your brother's fiancée.

3. You have a hankering to ride around in a limo all night.

4. You need to boogie-woogie with a male stripper.

5. The bride is dropping subtle hints: "Gee, a bachelorette party might be fun!"

6. Embarrassing your engaged friend a little sounds like a good time.

7. The whole wedding party needs to blow off some steam.

8. Did someone say "theme party"?

9. It's been too long since you've shown off your culinary skills.

10. The bride needs something to do while the bachelor party is going on.

Introduction

THERE ARE TWO TYPES of people in this world: Those who plan great parties, and those who don't. If you fall into the latter group, you may be thinking that you're just not up to the task. Maybe you're unorganized. Maybe you feel like you're just not creative enough. Maybe you've been to some really terrific parties and you feel like you could never duplicate the success of other hostesses—or maybe you've been to some truly awful gatherings and you're afraid that your own party would fall flat.

Relax. Hosting a party isn't brain surgery, though you will need an open mind, along with some basic organizational skills and maybe a little help from some friends. Bachelorette parties, in particular, are fun to host. There is very little etiquette written on bachelorette parties, which is great news for the hostess who's planning one, because you're restricted by very little. If you don't have a lot of party-planning experience, this is a great place to cut your teeth, so to speak.

Most bachelorette parties are all about having a good time, and hardly anyone will take you to task for putting out the wrong silverware. However, there are a few rules you'll have to abide by, like respecting the bride's wishes, respecting her guests, and if you've got a cohostess, working amicably with her.

While many—perhaps most—people think of bachelorette parties as orgiastic events where sparsely clothed men strut their stuff in the midst of ferocious women, this isn't always the case. The bachelorette party you plan may be a simple afternoon gathering for the bride, her family, and her friends; it may be a weekend in the country with the sorority sisters she seldom sees since graduation; it may be a dinner in a nice restaurant complete with tasteful gift-giving. It depends on what the bride wants, and your top priority as a hostess is being sensitive to her ideas and her wishes.

No matter what type of bachelorette party your engaged friend is looking for, this book will give you ideas and tips for planning a successful event. There are also party-planning basics, such as how to stick to your budget, how to get organized, and how to determine who should be on the guest list. Plus, you'll get helpful tips about handling potential trouble spots, like dealing with an overly obnoxious guest, what to do if someone else wants in on the hosting action, and making sure everyone gets around town and back home again safely.

The best thing a hostess can do is to keep calm and take an occasional deep breath. Remember: Cool-headed hostesses throw cool parties. In the event that something does go awry (for example, a snowstorm hits and only half your guests make it to the bachelorette party you've worked so hard to plan), you must bear in mind that the purpose of the party is to have fun. If you roll with the punches and keep your wits about you, your bride-to-be's bachelorette party is going to turn out great!

Chapter 1
A Little Background

Your friend or sister or cousin is engaged. You couldn't be happier for her, and she couldn't possibly be happier for herself. It's a wonderful time in her life, and you really want to do something special to commemorate it. How about throwing her a bachelorette party? It may be just the thing.

A Chance to Have Fun Together

Planning a wedding can be a very stressful time in a woman's life. In addition to all of the run-of-the-mill party-planning headaches, there's the emotional stress many brides experience. Mothers run amok. Caterers go out of business and disappear with deposits. Bridesmaids refuse to wear Spanish turquoise dresses.

At this time, the bride really needs to know that she has friends on her side. Throwing a bachelorette party for her will give her the chance to sit back and enjoy being the center of attention without lifting a finger.

She'll look back on this time of life and remember that in between her dress fittings and fighting with her mother over the wedding guest list, what she was really looking forward to was a night out with the girls—and she'll also remember she had a friend or two who thought so much of her that they planned a great party for her.

 ESSENTIAL

However your engaged friend feels, the bachelorette party is a great way to draw that proverbial line between singledom and married life. Especially if the bride-to-be is moving out of town after she gets married, it's nice to have an official acknowledgment of everything that's changing in her life *before* it all changes.

Ending an Era

Another reason brides like to have bachelorette parties is to officially say "so long" to their days of being a single woman. Some brides are sad or nostalgic to lose the freedoms of being single; others can't wait to be out of the dating pool.

No matter what age the bride-to-be is, spending some time with her friends before she becomes a wife is a good opportunity to reflect on what her friends have meant to her. Carrie, for example, is engaged to Rob, whom she will marry in a few months. Though they've been engaged for nearly two years, she is increasingly nervous as the Big Day draws nearer. "I'll be moving to Boston with Rob and leaving everything I've taken for granted—my friends and family, my job, my hometown," she says. "One minute, I can't wait to be with him, and the next minute, I can't stop crying."

The bride knows she has her groom's attention and support. Think of a bachelorette party as an opportunity to let her know she has yours, too. She may not have had time to think about how important her friendships are to her while she's been caught up in the cyclone of wedding preparations. And unlike a wedding atmosphere, a bachelorette party is often a smaller, more intimate gathering, giving the bride an opportunity to talk with every guest and really enjoy their company.

Giving Her a Big Sendoff

The bride-to-be is on the wedding track. The bachelorette party is likely to be her last stop before her big day. Consider how she's feeling. Many brides, although they're in love and ecstatic to be getting married, feel a little anxious and maybe even a little sad if they think they're going to lose their girlfriends and maybe even themselves, a little. A great way to assure her you're going to be there after she gets married is by throwing an unforgettable bachelorette party for her. She'll be reminded of why she likes you so much in the first place.

The Name of the Game Is Fun

Most brides become the center of attention if they plan a wedding of any size. In addition to being one of the two stars in her wedding production and being acknowledged as such by the florist, the caterer, the deejay, the dressmaker, and anyone else she's handing a check to, she will most likely be honored with a bridal shower or two.

 ALERT!

Make sure you're on the same page as your friend. Unless you're planning a surprise bachelorette party, get some input from the bride-to-be about what kind of party she'd like. It may be possible that what you have in mind is too wild for her.

However, being a star can be stressful. The bachelorette party is an opportunity for the bride to do something different, and for the following reasons:

- Bachelorette parties tend to be laid-back affairs.
- The focus is on the bride and her pals just having a good time.
- No one needs to wear her Sunday best.
- No one needs to bring her Sunday manners.
- The guest list may be more exclusive.

Not everyone needs to know about the bride's wild side. The bachelorette party is a chance for the bride-to-be to show her true colors—a side of her that Aunt Marjorie may not ever want to see.

So whatever kind of party you and the bride decide on, the focus has to be on the bride enjoying herself. At this party, she doesn't have to stress over the color of the tablecloths or whether she's received one toaster or two. The bride should be able to think of this as a proverbial breath of fresh air.

Combination Shower/ Bachelorette Party

Unfortunately, in this busy world, not everything always goes according to plan. The bride's wedding day may be fast approaching, and suddenly someone points out that she hasn't had a shower—nor is anyone currently putting one together for her.

If you're a bridesmaid, a wedding shower is something you and the other girls in the wedding party should have thought of and planned for. Luckily, all is not lost. Why not organize a quick little event that's a wedding shower and bachelorette party all rolled into one? It's a great way to combine the two events and get you off the hook. If you plan it well enough, the bride may even think that this was your intention all along.

 FACT

> A wedding shower is a lovely tradition; showers tend to be afternoon luncheon affairs where everyone remains on their best behavior at all times. There is lots of gift-giving and compliments, and often a wedding shower is a surprise party for the bride.

Another great reason to combine the two parties is if the bride lives out of town and is returning home briefly—hosting a joint shower and bachelorette party will save her some time.

Allison found herself in such a situation when she was in her friend Maria's wedding. "Maria and I live in New York, hundreds of miles away from her family. New York is really Maria's home—she's lived here since college, and all of her friends are here. She doesn't even go to her family's home for the holidays.

"I don't know why I never thought to host a shower

for her. I guess I didn't read the wedding etiquette books. But we were getting down to the wire, and I realized there wasn't enough time to have a shower and a bachelorette party—so we had one big party. I invited her family, of course. It was pretty toned-down because her family's very serious, but Maria got her shower and her bachelorette party, and she was ecstatic. I hate to think what would have happened if I had completely dropped the ball on this one."

An Equal-Opportunity Affair

If you're thinking of rolling these two parties into one, divide time equally between the events. Have your shower-time early on in the evening, with gift-giving and polite conversation around the punch bowl; after the gifts and cake you can easily segue into a lighter, less formal setting by putting on some fun music and spiking the punch in that bowl. Every guest wins in this situation: Those who want to stay and party will, and those who aren't completely comfortable with bachelorette parties are free to go.

It's important to make it clear on the invitations that this is a dual party. You don't want to infuriate the bride's grandmother by springing a bachelorette party on her when she arrives for the shower. She may be less than thrilled with the whole idea. Give her a chance to opt out.

Also, make sure you aren't kicking anyone out too early. Asking guests to attend a shower with a gift and then rushing through it so the young folks can get down to bachelorette business is completely unacceptable. Give yourself a minimum of two hours for the shower portion of the event.

 ALERT!

If you do happen to find yourself killing two parties with one invitation, don't skimp on the event. You'll add insult to injury if you have been lax in your duties—and then cut corners on the party you do give. The bride will absolutely notice, and if you intend to have her in your own wedding someday, you can expect the same treatment from her.

Putting the Family Puzzle Back Together

Life is crazy in this day and age. People are so busy that they sometimes forget to keep in touch with their families. They drift apart, literally and figuratively. Or, sadly, a little family misunderstanding can get blown up into a huge affair, where sisters or mothers and daughters don't speak to each other for weeks . . . or months . . . or even years.

Here's your situation: Your friend is getting married and her family is a little *off* (and that's being kind). Her sister hasn't spoken to her in six years because of a recipe-stealing incident. (Hey, what was wrong with the bride selling her late Aunt Edna's top-secret meatball recipe anyway? Edna certainly can't use it anymore, the bride needed to pay her rent, and that new Italian restaurant needed a signature dish.)

Inviting the sister to a bridal shower is required, of course. However, in the event that scores of women-folk—the same ones who will be at the shower—have heard about the great Meatball Caper, it might be very uncomfortable—or impossible—for either the bride or the sister to take those first baby steps toward reconciliation at such a formal event. If the sister is at all aware of the possibility of every guest watching her every move so that she and/or the bride can be analyzed later for sport, she may choose not to come to the shower at all—no matter how much she wants to see her sister.

 ESSENTIAL

If the bride-to-be has been distant while plan-ning her wedding, a night out on the town may be exactly what she needs to remind her that she's most likely not going to live alone with her groom on the Island of Wedded Bliss forever—she's going to need her friends even after she signs the marriage license.

A tentative reconciliation is better achieved in a more relaxed setting, like the bachelorette party you're giving. Inviting the sister to the bachelorette is *not* required, which makes it something of a more welcoming gesture.

The sister will realize that someone actually invited her because she's wanted there, not because she's a relative (like the other eighty women at the shower), and not because the bride wants a place setting from her.

The contrast between the two settings is dramatic. Picture what could happen if the sister shows up to the shower, expecting to make amends (or to start the process, anyway) with the bride—and the bride is too busy greeting and chatting with other guests, and oohing and ahhing over her gifts. She realistically can't spend a huge block of time with her long-lost sibling, or *any* one person, at the shower. This might actually make matters worse, in the event that the sister is really insecure and/or a little more off than you thought.

Including her in the less-demanding affair, where the bride will actually have time to talk and reconnect with her, may work wonders. Don't be reluctant to give this a shot. After all, a big part of weddings is the bride taking stock of the relationships in her life. On the other hand, don't throw the sister into the mix without clearing it with the bride first—you don't want the fallout from that landing solely on you.

Bachelors and Bachelorettes

Bachelorette parties are relatively recent phenomena, a feminist-era response to bachelor parties, which have a long history and reputation for being less-than-respectable affairs. We've all heard the tales. Joe Groom got so inebriated at his bachelor party that he ended up missing his wedding. Or Mr. Prince Charming had a fling with Ms. Exotic Dancer who was hired to entertain the guests at his testosterone-fueled blast.

Women no longer feel the need to sit home and count the days, hours, and minutes until they walk down the aisle. They're looking for a little fun, and—darn it—they're going to find some. In fact, bachelorette parties can get just as wild and crazy. But does this mean that a bachelorette party must adhere to those same standards? Not at all.

Girls, Girls, Girls

The great thing about bachelorette parties being a somewhat recent invention is that there's less tradition to depend on and refer to, so women are forging ahead and blazing their own bachelorette trails.

 FACT

A bachelorette party is all about women doing what they're comfortable with—it shouldn't be seen as a battle of the sexes to see which gender can do the wildest, and often dumbest, things. Any party that has such a competition as its foundation is bound to end up getting out of hand, and fast!

Bachelorettes shouldn't even attempt to be carbon copies of bachelor parties. This is strictly a woman thing, and should be celebrated as such. Some things you may want to have on hand that will clearly designate this as a girls' night include a gaudy, fake veil for the bride to wear; garish pillbox hats for the bridesmaids; and pictures or embarrassing stories about the bride. You can bet the groom and his friends won't be engaging in such fun silliness at the bachelor party.

There's no denying that female friendships are some of the most enduring and strongest relationships in a woman's life. A bachelorette party acknowledges the fact that although the bride may only have eyes for her groom, real life continues to swirl around her. Unfortunately, some brides lose touch with their girlfriends as soon as they snag the engagement ring. A bachelorette party is just the thing to mend any bridges that may have fallen into disrepair over the engagement period.

Do It Your Own Way

Women tend to think of bachelorette parties as more of a time to connect with their female friends before the wedding, and not so much as a last opportunity to get cozy with another man. That's not to say that a half-naked male dancer won't be included—but it's safe to assume he will be kept at arm's length.

Nancy, who was married last year, commented on her bachelorette party and compared it to her husband, Steve's, bachelor bash: "My bachelorette party consisted of twelve girls. We went out, cruising bars in a limo, getting drunk and silly. We went to a dance club and screamed at the male dancers, but the whole time we were giggling and so far removed from the sexuality of the place . . . we could have been on the street, and we would have acted the same way. It was about us feeding off each other and acting crazy.

"Steve's friends, meanwhile, took him to a strip joint—where they spent the entire evening. They got drunk, they paid for lap dances, and they basically spent the night looking at naked women—up close and very personally. I was so offended and hurt, I cried for days. How could he do that when we were getting married in two weeks?"

Dealing with the Party-Pooper Groom

Some grooms are just not all that supportive of the bachelorette party. This is especially curious when the groom is planning on indulging in a traditional bachelor party, complete with multiple kegs and breasts galore.

 ALERT!

If you find yourself in a similar situation, remember: It's not up to you to judge the relationship between the betrothed couple. In fact, their relationship is strictly off limits to your comments.

Even when the bride comes weeping to you about how unfair her fiancé can be, zip that lip. You can always be supportive of her and give her some sympathy, but you should never, ever call him names or offer your own insights into his personality. You're playing a dangerous game of Monkey in the Middle, and you're about to find out who the monkey is.

Regardless of your feelings about the groom, she has chosen him for her life partner, and if she doesn't want to rock the boat, don't rock it for her. Following that logic, you should leave it up to the bride to decide if she wants a wild bash, a quiet gathering, or any bachelorette party at all. This is always the bride's decision, but in this situation, it's *extremely* important for you to follow her wishes to the letter.

If she wants one stripper, don't hire three. If she doesn't want fake penises decorating her party, don't buy them. Again, this is all common sense, but you're wading in potentially treacherous waters here.

Now, if she's determined to have the bachelorette party many women imagine, complete with flowing alcohol, phallic decorations, and sweaty, writhing male dancers, that's her prerogative. You are considerably less responsible for any friction that will result when the overprotective groom hears about it, though you will probably bear the brunt of any accusations and anger the groom expresses after the fact.

Just like so many other planning pitfalls, you could very well run into a *very* sticky situation here. What if, for example, your brother is the jealous groom? Or what if the groom is your best male friend and the bride, who is your best female friend, wants a bachelorette party he won't sanction? What is a hostess to do?

No, crying is not the answer. You basically have two choices here. You can bow out as hostess, or you can be the hostess who incurs the groom's wrath. Neither choice looks very attractive from this angle, but unfortunately, this is reality. You have to weigh the options and decide whom you would rather have a little angry with you—the bride or the groom.

FACT

> The whole industry of bachelor and bachelorette parties is steeped in sex. For example, an Internet search for bachelorette information turns up Web site after Web site laden with sex toys, sex games, and snacks in the shape of male genitalia. Maybe this is exactly what you're after; maybe it's not.

A Word of Warning

It would be unrealistic to think that bachelorette parties are filled with wholesome activities, though some are completely innocent affairs. It's an occasion where the bride gets to let loose and have fun with the girls. Just make sure that what you're planning fits in with what you're willing to take responsibility for. You are the hostess, and this party will reflect on you. Just because men sometimes feel the need to make unintelligent choices about bachelor party activities doesn't mean women have to follow suit.

If the bride-to-be is bound and determined to match the traditional male revelry—that is, she's looking for a "last fling"—and you're aware of this, have a heart-to-heart chat with her. Not only will the results be disastrous, but as the hostess of this event, you'll be smack dab in the middle of the trouble when it hits. (And it will hit.) That's where the fun ends.

Stick to Good, Clean Fun

Bachelor and/or bachelorette parties can easily make the transition from harmless fun to offensive, hurtful actions, whether intended or not. Where that line is drawn is up to the bride and groom. Your job as the hostess is to keep the party on the correct side of the line.

If you're having trouble assessing the appropriateness of a situation you find yourself in, ask yourself: Is this something that is totally out of character for the bride? Is this something you're completely uncomfortable with? Even if you are the only sober one with any thought capabilities at this point, don't just follow the crowd. Speak up.

Remember that the bachelorette party is supposed to be fun. While you should absolutely steer away from being a party pooper, you shouldn't feel bad about being the voice of reason if things are obviously spiraling out of control. Sometimes that's a fine line, but if you keep an eye on things, you'll be able to spot the first signs of trouble.

Chapter 2

The Bachelorette Party Hostess

Now that you've read more about what a bachelorette party is, you probably have one of two reactions. Either you're already planning a wild, nutty bachelorette night for your friend, or you're dreading the thought of it. What if the bride's very particular sister wants to be the hostess? Or, what if you don't know the bride that well? Can you still have a hand in the planning *and* live to tell the tale? This chapter will cover some hostess basics and give you an opportunity to test your Hostess IQ.

Who's Throwing This Shindig, Anyway?

The biggest issue to be resolved is who is going to play hostess of the bachelorette party. Bridesmaids are an obvious choice, but keep in mind that they're already most likely spending big bucks on their wedding attire, not to mention they're also expected to host a shower— all this in addition to any travel expenses they incur during these events.

 QUESTION?

Can I host a bachelorette party even though I'm not in the wedding party?
While traditionally bridesmaids are responsible for hosting the bachelorette party, remember that they are also in charge of hosting a bridal shower. Assuming you want to do it, it's absolutely acceptable for you to offer to take control of the bachelorette party for your engaged friend, even if you're not in the wedding party.

You do not have to be a member of the wedding party to host a bachelorette party. If you're the bride's good pal, that's enough. Even if you find yourself in the position of throwing a bachelorette party for a bride you aren't all that close to—say, your future sister-in-law—the best reason to do it is a sincere desire to honor the bride and show her a good time. You needn't know her for twenty years to want to throw her a party.

Why You Should Get Involved

The poor bride! As her wedding day approaches, she looks more worn out than excited. She's been poked by the dressmaker's pins, forced to taste wedding cake that she swears was decades old, and has practically signed over her first and second child just to book the reception hall.

What she really needs is to let loose. That's where you come in, saving the day with a bang-up bachelorette party she'll never forget—that is, if she remembers it at all. The entire point of a bachelorette party is to indulge the bride in one last pre-wedding caper. You may think she's been pampered plenty, what with all the attention she's been getting as of late, but this is different. She doesn't have to get dolled up for this party; she just has to show up and have a blast.

Giving Her a Little Love

Maybe you and the bride have been friends for years and have been through the trials and joys of graduations, gross apartments, great and lousy boyfriends, and new jobs and other experiences. Or maybe this is a relatively new friend you want to host a party for, someone you've met in your adult life and whom you've clicked with because she's smart and funny and is really going places.

Whatever the case, you obviously think a lot of her to want to give her a big sendoff into marriage. Instead of handing her a congratulatory greeting card—you can do that when she gets her next big promotion—make her the center of attention at her bachelorette party.

Welcome to the Family

Your brother—the one who tortured you throughout adolescence, the one you swore would never turn out to be a normal person, the one you're almost certain sold your socks to that creepy guy who had a crush on you—has found himself a fiancée. Not only are you completely shocked that he's decided to settle down, you're also amazed that his future wife seems to be a great girl. You actually *like* her.

 FACT

In a situation where you're hosting a party for someone you don't know very well—like your brother's fiancée—get some information on what type of party she expects and plan your party accordingly. A boisterous woman may actually prefer a quiet evening at home. Likewise, a seemingly shy girl may be itching to let her wild side out.

What better way to welcome her to the fold than hosting a bachelorette party for her? If she's the awesome person you think she is, she'll fit right in with your sisters and your female cousins. She'll be the main attraction at a party your family wants to give her—and the best part is that because this is an optional thing (a bachelorette party is really a nice extra for most women in their pre-wedding schedules), she'll appreciate it all the more.

No Need to Fret

One of the best points about bachelorette parties is that you aren't going to feel the same type of pressure as you would if you were planning a very formal event. This party can be as informal, and as unstructured as you want. Does the bride want to play some party games? Great. Does she think party games are lame? No problem, there won't be any. Because bachelorette parties tend to be unique parties that cater to the bride's personality and her wishes, very few people will arrive holding a list of things they expect to happen at the party you're hosting.

That's not to say that you should attempt to throw this, or any party, together in a day. You do have an obligation as the hostess—to the bride and to the guests. Get organized, plan something fun, and let the good times roll.

Being There in Spirit

Alas, despite your best efforts and your dreams of cohosting the bachelorette party for your best friend, you just can't make it from Miami to San Francisco for the party. Life is like that sometimes. All is not lost, however. You can always be there in spirit by sending the bride a little reminder of yourself and your friendship.

Gina could not make it to Barb's bachelorette party. Gina, who was working in London, was coming to the wedding in New York in four weeks' time, and it just was not feasible for her to make two trips across the Atlantic. To lighten the sense of sadness the two friends felt, Gina wrote a little note to Barb, reminding her of all the crazy things they had done as teenagers—which inadvertently also pointed out how much Barb had changed and matured since those days—and she included some funny pictures of the two of them in full prom regalia.

Barb says: "I had no idea this was coming. Gina sent it to one of our friends who was throwing the party, and she read it out loud and passed these hysterical pictures around. It was such a hit, and I felt so happy that Gina did that for me. It really was like she was there with us."

You can send your spirit off to the bride in many ways. Send the bride a bottle of wine or flowers the day of the party. Make her a CD of her favorite music from her young days that she can play at the party (and afterwards, too). Give her a call and let her know one more time that you're thinking of her and you'll be seeing her soon at the wedding.

If you can't see yourself sending the bride a sentimental keepsake, send her something else, like a suggestive game for her and her groom to play or a gift certificate for the massage she could use to alleviate her unrelenting pre-wedding tension.

 ESSENTIAL

Keep in mind that you shouldn't feel actual prolonged guilt about missing the party. If you've done all you can and you can't make it, chalk it up to bad timing. If the bride is threatening never to speak to you again if you miss her bachelorette party, remind yourself that she is stressed out and may regret her actions later.

Don't Step on Anyone's Toes

While you may be bursting to throw your engaged coworker an unforgettable bash, consider that others may feel the same way. If she has a sister or a close relative, one of them may already be planning a bachelorette party for her, especially if she is in the wedding party.

The best way to avoid overstepping boundaries and hard feelings (after all, this is supposed to be fun for everyone) is by establishing clear lines of communication. Don't assume the bride's sister *isn't* planning a bachelorette party just because you haven't personally heard anything about it. By the same token, don't assume she *is* planning a party just because she's the maid of honor.

Put your phone to use and make a call. (You always knew there was a reason you signed up for 500 free minutes.) If there's a potential miscommunication, it will be averted in moments. You may save the day, if, for example, no party is in the works and the bride is really looking forward to having one.

 ALERT!

Don't wait for someone else to take the initiative on organizing the bachelorette party, especially if the wedding date is right around the corner. Everyone else may also be assuming it's taken care of. As a result, the bride could be left high and dry, not to mention angry and hurt.

Hosting Together

If it turns out that there is more than one person who's itching to play hostess, it can work to your benefit in a huge way. Two or more hostesses are always better than one, as long as you manage to agree on how the party should be run.

Keep in mind that planning any party involves a budget, invitations, some sort of entertainment, preparing a menu, and choosing a location. These are the bare basics of party planning. If you're planning a large bachelorette party and you have considerable party-planning experience, great. If, on the other hand, the biggest soiree you've put together was last Sunday's dinner at your house—and the only other guest was your reflection in the window—you might want to consider sharing the duties of this party. If some unforeseen catastrophe strikes—like you've booked reservations at a restaurant that suddenly goes out of business—you'll have another person to depend on and help you with contingency plans. It never hurts to have an extra set of hands, and you'll be learning how to plan a large party in the meantime.

Dueling Hostesses

If, on the other hand, you are one of two or more women vying for the title of hostess but none of you can agree on anything, you may want to back off. Planning an event like this requires working together. One of you can't decide, for example, to have the bachelorette party in someone's tiny apartment in order to keep costs down while someone else is deciding to invite 100 people and serve lobster tails. Even though you're all trying to please the bride, this alone does not guarantee success in the planning arena.

 ESSENTIAL

You don't want to be an ignorant hostess. Before you move forward into planning and organizing, find out what you might not already know about hosting a bachelorette party.

Pairing up with someone who has a completely different plan is guaranteed to cause you sleepless nights and a whole lot of aggravation, not to mention the bickering and lingering resentment you'll also experience. There's nothing wrong with going separate ways and planning two bachelorette parties for the bride.

(Almost) Family Feuding

In the same vein, imagine this scenario: Though you have generously offered to host the bachelorette party, you're now in a tug-of-war over control of the party with the bride's sister, who heard that you were honing in on what she considers to be her territory. Unfortunately, the sister is the biggest control freak you have ever known in your life. The bride, in contrast, is superme-llow. Or maybe it's the other way around: The bride has definite ideas of how she wants her bachelorette party to be, and her sister has no clue how to plan for it and is procrastinating in her preparations. Either way, the sister's vision is very different from the bride's, and you sense a party disaster looming on the horizon. What are you going to do now?

Your choices are simple: Work with the sister or get out now. One option is to throw a separate bachelorette party for the bride—the one she *really* wants—and let the sister host her own. The bride gets two parties, and she won't be unhappy about that. She will be unhappy, how- ever, if the sister kicks you out as hostess and as a result she gets a party that is the complete opposite of what she wanted. Hang in there for her; she'll really appreciate the effort you've made.

 FACT

While it's perfectly fine for a bride to have two bachelorette parties if you and another hostess can't agree on logistics, more than two is excessive. Your friend is getting married. She's not moving to Jupiter.

Before You Get Started

You want to host a bachelorette party for your friend, but you've never done this kind of thing before. Before you get into the initial stages of planning, you should know there are a few rules of etiquette that will govern your every move. It's not as complicated or stringent as it sounds, and actually most of these rules are based on common sense.

 Take the Bachelorette Party Quiz

Before you get started, how about taking this quiz to find out how much you already know and what you need to find out? Find yourself a pencil, take a deep breath, and good luck! And if you don't know the answers—not to worry. These situations are all covered in this book.

1. The bride is getting married for the second time. Is it acceptable to host a bachelorette party for her?

    a. No way. She's already had her fun.
    b. Yes, but it should be limited to a small gathering.
    c. The bride-to-be still deserves an all-out party, even if it won't be her first.

The answer depends on your relationship with the bride, but generally speaking, it's fine to give her a great big bachelorette party again, as long as she's comfortable with the idea.

2. The bride wants a bevy of strippers at her bachelorette party, and the budget only allows for one. What should you do?

    a. Go for broke—it's her big night.
    b. Tell her it's one or nothing.
    c. Say nothing, do nothing, and ignore the issue altogether—this is no time for conflict.

You know the answer. It's "one or nothing." Of course, you're going to say it a little more nicely, and explain your budget issues to the bride. Ignoring the issue isn't going to help, and neither will paying out the nose for something you can't afford. When your rent is due and you're broke, you can't offer up Rocky Balbimbo, the dancer who comes out swinging, as payment to your landlord.

3. On the night of the party, some of your guests are highly dismayed at all the hoopla and overt sexual tone of the party you're hosting. They're trying to mellow things out. (Read: They're party poopers and they're trying to deflate Bob, the blow-up doll.) What should you do?

    a. Kick them out.
    b. Have a little chat with them.
    c. Leave it up to the bride.

Either talk to them or leave it up to the bride. See if you can ask the bride first—maybe she wouldn't mind toning things down a bit, especially if it's late in the evening, or the distressed guest is a relative of hers and she wants to keep the peace.

If that isn't the case, you're up to bat. Tell the party poopers politely that this is the party the bride wanted to have, that they're making her feel bad, and to please cease and desist. If they get angry, they'll probably just leave and let the party continue.

4. The bride wants to invite her family to the bachelorette party. The girls who are hosting it want to have a night of drinking and partying. Can you put a time limit on how long the bride's grandmother sticks around?

a. Yes.
b. No.
c. No, but it can be accomplished by giving the family lots of little hints—like mentioning how much you're all going to drink once they leave.

This is basic politeness—obviously, the answer is a flat "no." You cannot put a time limit on how long particular guests can stay. And dropping hints about how much fun you'd be having if only they would leave is incredibly rude. If you're inviting them to the bachelorette party, remember it's at the bride's request—this is her night, not yours.

5. You've just received an odd call from the groom, asking you for specific details about the bachelorette party. What do you tell him?

a. "No speaky the English," hoping that he thinks he mistakenly dialed someone in Chile.
b. You spill your guts and tell him everything, from what you're serving at your house to what time you're all hitting the bars later in the evening.
c. You refer him to his bride.

This answer is dependent on several factors, but it's usually best to avoid giving him all the information and instead refer him to the bride. If they're having some sort of disagreement over her bachelorette party, she may not be sharing all the details of it with him. Stay on the sidelines for this one.

6. You're going nuts the night of the party. Nothing's gone right. The limo is stranded somewhere thirty miles away with a flat tire, your crab cakes are burned, and someone drank the entire bottle of vodka—and it's only 9 P.M. What's your move?

   a. Apologize to everyone and send them home.
   b. Go out and get some more vodka and appetizers.
   c. Take a deep breath and roll with it.

This is actually a trick question. The best answer is just to take a deep breath and roll with it. You can't do anything about the limo at this time—cross your fingers and hope that tire gets fixed. However, if you've planned for any eventuality, you've got plenty of backup liquor and snacks, so you can stay in all night if need be.

7. You're going to have the bachelorette party in a restaurant, and there are only seven girls going. Do you need to call ahead?

    a. Only on a weekend night.
    b. No—you're a small party.
    c. Only if you're planning to have a stripper crash the party.

The answer depends on the type of restaurant you're planning to attend and when you're planning to go there. If you're going to any restaurant on a busy night or any restaurant that requires reservations, you should call ahead, unless you want to wait two hours for a table. If you're going to a chain restaurant on a Tuesday night, there's really no need to call ahead. However, you should always call and check to see if male dancers are welcome, even if they're not going to eat anything.

8. The bride doesn't drink, but most of the guests you're inviting to the bachelorette party do. Is it all right to serve alcohol?

    a. Yes.
    b. No.
    c. Only if you hide it from the bride.

Unless the bride is a recovering alcoholic and she met all of her invited guests at group meetings of the Alcoholics Anonymous, it's fine for you to serve alcohol. Guests will expect it at a bachelorette party. However, make sure to stock your bar evenly—have plenty of juice and soda on hand for the bride.

The Results

So, how did you do? If you got one or two answers wrong, don't worry, especially if you're a first-time hostess. If you found yourself comparing your answer to the correct one and saying, "What?!" time and time again, you may need to adjust your thinking a bit. The bachelorette party is about the bride and the guests. Your job—and it's not necessarily a glamorous one—is to keep everyone happy. You can do it! Keep reading.

Chapter 3

Get the
Ball Rolling

Once you sign on as hostess, you're the Go-To Girl. Planning a party involves a lot of coordination and organization. If you lack these characteristics in your normal day-to-day life, you're going to find yourself frustrated when you've lost the guest list for the umpteenth time. In this chapter, you'll find hints on how to keep yourself lucid when you feel as though you're trapped in a party-planning nightmare.

Calm Those Hostess Jitters

If this is the first sizable party you've ever thrown, you may be feeling a little anxious. The larger the party, the better chance you're going to want to split up the host duties, if only for financial reasons. There are very few people who are willing and able to take on the cost of renting a hall, paying for the food, drinks, entertainment, and decorations. It's just not practical. A smaller party is much more realistic for a single host.

Stay Organized

Party planning involves so many details that your best plan of attack—and the best way to prevent major problems—is getting organized. Buy several different colored folders and label them—one for food ideas, one for the guest list, one for entertainment options, and so on. Find an accessible spot for them and keep them there for easy reference. Each time you sign a contract or even receive a brochure, make sure you save it in the appropriate folder. This way you'll know exactly where everything is and you'll be able to tell ABC Entertainment, for example, that yes, you *did* send the deposit for the karaoke machine, because you have the canceled check right there in your red "entertainment" folder. Problem averted.

You'll also want to have a notebook to make a note of such calls (including whom you speak with, the time, and date) and to keep yourself on track so that you'll remember to call and confirm that the karaoke machine will be arriving on time. Or else you may have to listen to the bride's cousin singing a cappella, and no one will find that entertaining.

 ESSENTIAL

> When making any sort of business arrangement, make sure to get the name of the person you're dealing with, as well as any other pertinent details of the conversation. You want to be able to say that on April 4, for example, Joe Schmoe quoted you a significantly lower price than you're being offered now, two weeks later.

One final tip: Being a hostess is not for the meek. You will find yourself having to be an assertive person in order to run a successful show. You may be handling reservations, caterers, entertainment options, transportation—and trying to coordinate everything while keeping costs under control. At the very least, you will be responsible for keeping your guests happy and manageable (if someone has had too much of the bubbly, for example). Put on your toughest skin and prepare to be Superhostess.

Consider the Bride-to-Be

After you calm your hostess jitters, the next step you need to take is evaluating what kind of bachelorette party the bride actually wants. This is a crucial step. Remember, this party is for her. (If you haven't had your own bachelorette party yet, hand this book to a good friend or your sister when you get engaged. Highlight this section. You'll get the bachelorette party you want *then*.) First off, there are several bridal types to consider.

The Bride Who's Gone Crazy

It's an unfortunate fact that some engaged women lose their heads once they start planning a wedding, and perhaps even more so as their big day draws near. You want to handle this type of bride with extreme caution, as she has definite ideas about how things ought to be and will most likely explode if something goes awry.

 QUESTION?

What if the bride and I just can't agree on the bachelorette party?
In that case, consider dropping the whole thing. Some brides are very hard to please and no matter what you do, it won't be enough. Rather than ruin the friendship completely because she berates the party you're planning, gracefully and nicely bow out as soon as possible, so that someone else can take over.

If the bride-to-be in your life is experiencing extreme anxiety, moodiness, and has suddenly turned into a control freak, you'll want to plan a low-key party. The less complicated the plans, the less chance that things will go horribly wrong. Suggest to her a nice dinner out with the girls. This will place your party in an environment that you personally have limited control over. She can't blame you, for example, if the napkins aren't folded just right. Of course, this doesn't mean that you should stand back and watch her freak out all over the waitress, either, but the waitress has a big advantage over you—she can walk away from your friend. She can even hand your friend over to someone else. You, unfortunately, cannot.

The main thing you want to avoid with this type of bride is setting yourself up for failure. You're giving her a party to celebrate her marriage. You don't want to end up not speaking to her because she's being demonic.

Also keep in mind that she's supposed to work *with* you, which means she should acknowledge the budget for her bachelorette party, as well as the time that you have available for planning it. Yes, you want to accommodate her wishes, but you have to keep your expenditures and sanity in check, too. She can't demand a Bachelorette Ball, for example, when the budget is leading you more toward planning a small party at your pad. Just because you want a little input from her doesn't mean she gets to walk all over you.

The Second Timer

Maybe your friend is getting married for the second time . . . or third . . . or fourth. She wants another bachelorette party, but you're just not sure if it's appropriate. If this is the case, don't worry. As long as the bride is comfortable with the idea, there's really no reason not to give her a bachelorette party, even if it's not her first wedding.

 ALERT!

> With the second timer, you may encounter that you are running short on guests. Fair or not, people start to tire of attending the pre-wedding events (not to mention weddings) of the same person, over and over.

Keep in mind that your friend may not want the exact same kind of bachelorette party she had the first time around, especially if she's considerably older. She may be looking for more of a girly get-together time, maybe in a bar, maybe with a few drinks, but not necessarily with a blow-up doll chained to her wrist. Of course, your first move is to talk to the bride. She can shed all kinds of light on how she wants you to proceed with the party planning.

The Conservative Bride

If your engaged friend is a little shy, or quiet, or just generally likes things scaled back, think twice—and then think again—before planning a wild bachelorette party for her. Chances are, it will make her uncomfortable, despite the fact that other guests may enjoy bar hopping or visiting male dance clubs.

Sometimes quiet women really *do* enjoy letting loose in the company of their girlfriends, but you shouldn't assume that such is the case with your bride. Ask her what she wants—and then listen carefully. Again, it's important to keep in mind that this is not a party for you and your girlfriends—it's for the bride-to-be. She'll notice if you're trying to commandeer her engagement and are using it as an excuse to party all night while she'd rather be somewhere else.

The Laid-back Bride

This woman will usually go along with whatever you want to do. It may be that she's so overwhelmed by her wedding planning that she just doesn't want to think about anything else. Or it may be that she's simply grateful that you're giving her a party and doesn't want to tell you what to do. Or maybe she really wants everyone to have a fun time and wants to leave it up to the group consensus.

Whatever the case, she's giving you carte blanche to do what you want. Talking with the other guests is an option here. Or maybe you have a specific type of party in mind. Whatever you decide, you've been given the green light to do what you feel is appropriate.

FACT

> Even if you're dealing with a laid-back type, you should still consider what things the bride-to-be might be really uncomfortable with and avoid them. If she doesn't like to boogie, for example, don't plan on cruising dance clubs all night.

The Bride Who Wants Nothing

This bride may be morally opposed to bachelorette parties, or perhaps she and her fiancé have had enough of the pre-wedding events. Maybe she's just too busy and can't find time to fit a bachelorette party into her schedule. Don't force a party on her. If she really doesn't want one and you plan one anyway, she'll show up grudgingly, if at all, and she may even be angry about it, especially if she's made her wishes clear.

Again, don't try to use her engagement as an excuse to have a party she doesn't want. If you just love having parties and you're itching to have everyone over, go ahead. But make it clear it's *your* party. Don't label it as an occasion to honor her.

The Bride You Hardly Know

You've been asked to plan a bachelorette party for your brother's fiancée. This is a tricky situation, because you barely know the girl. Every time you've spoken with her, you've both been on your best behavior. You have no idea if she's a wild child or a schoolmarm at heart. And to top it off, you kind of resent having to give her a party when you think her sister, who lives ten miles away, should be doing it. But your brother has asked you to do this, and if you say no, you're just a great big meany, right?

Well, not necessarily. Since she's going to be family, you should make every effort to accommodate your brother's request, but if you have severe budget restraints and it's going to be a hardship, you must explain this.

 ESSENTIAL

> You shouldn't ever feel obligated to host a party, especially for someone you really don't know. If you decline, it's possible someone will be unhappy, but you shouldn't lose your shirt just so your brother's fiancée can have a party.

It's possible, though, that you are interested in throwing a party for your soon-to-be sister-in-law. Your budget can handle the expenses of hosting a bachelorette party and you want to welcome her to the family. Sometimes it's very hard to get a handle on someone's true colors and wishes, even after addressing specific issues with her—like whether she would like a wild party or something more quiet. If she's been supersweet and seems reserved but you think that deep down she's as uninhibited as they come, err on the side of caution—please! If she really is conservative, nothing will get you off on the wrong foot faster than hosting a party where everyone brings her a gift of sleazy lingerie. That's a bridge you won't be able to cross back over.

Caroline made this mistake when she was asked to cohost a bachelorette party for her cousin Denny's fiancée together with Denny's sisters. "The bride seemed so *good* that the rest of us thought it had to be an act for the family," Caroline says, perspiring a little even as she recalls the incident. "She seemed like she had a really great sense of humor. So my cousins and I threw her this bachelorette party with all of these really suggestive decorations. . . . The bride and her sister walked in, took a look, and her sister walked out and never came back.

 ALERT!

Matching the party type to the bride's personality and/or wishes is absolutely imperative. You can't host a wild evening for a reserved woman, and likewise you shouldn't try to have a subdued party for a party animal. Your party will be a flop with the most important guest, the bride-to-be.

"The bride stuck it out for a little while, but when the other girls started passing around the big toys we had bought for centerpieces, she left, too. Denny was furious with us. Now his wife barely acknowledges me at family things."

Though this seems like an extreme reaction, it's an example of what can happen if someone is uncomfortable with a bachelorette party that has a racy theme. If deep, deep down, she really is a wild woman and you give her a tame bachelorette party, she won't hold it against you. You'll all laugh one day about how innocent you thought she was.

The Bride Who Wants It All

This is the bride who wants action, and she wants it right now—or at least before she skips down the aisle. She's up for a wild night of drinking, dancing, questionable game playing, odd cuisine—cookies in all kinds of suggestive shapes, anyone?—and a male dancer dressed, albeit only briefly, as a butler. Don't question her tastes. Just indulge her.

Though this bride is pretty easygoing, you may have to get your rear in gear and do a whole lot of planning. Those cookies aren't going to make themselves, you know, and the games won't be planning themselves. And the stripper definitely isn't going to show up without you calling him. You can read more on planning a party like this in Chapter 7, but for now, plan to plan.

What Are My Responsibilities?

No one wants to come to a party that has obviously been thrown together at the last minute, least of all the guest of honor. Now that you know what your bride-to-be has in mind for her bachelorette party, it's time to start getting organized and plan, plan, plan. Be prepared for anything, and your party is sure to be a success.

Finding a Structure

Depending on the size of gathering you're planning, you may have very little or a lot to concern yourself with. When planning a large gathering, you need to get organized before you make even one little party plan. Here are some things to consider:

- Your budget (which will affect everything else on this list)
- The guest list
- Timing
- Activities/entertainment
- Location
- Menu
- Decorations
- Gifts

Everything on this list will give your party some sort of design, and you can plan from there. If you're working on a tight budget, for example, you may want to host a party at home with simple decorations (if any), music from your own stereo for entertainment, and appetizers from your own kitchen. If your budget is substantial, though, you may opt to have the party at a restaurant where a caterer will provide the food and a deejay will provide entertainment for dozens of guests.

 ESSENTIAL

Budget dictates *everything* when planning a party. Determine what you are willing to bankroll for this party and stay within your parameters. Don't go broke trying to do something nice for your friend. She wouldn't want that.

Get to Work

Planning a party sounds easy enough. After all, the party's going to be a blast, so planning it shouldn't be so hard, right? Well, that depends on several factors, including your previous hosting experience, the effort you're willing to put into it, and your level of organization.

All of these factors are dependent on one another. Even if you've hosted more parties than you can count, your next bash can still go bust if you just don't feel like doing it or if you've lost all your paperwork—such as the all-important reservation number for the block of hotel rooms you've booked. Likewise, this may be the first party you're giving for someone else; but if you're organized and enthusiastic, you're more likely to have a successful event.

FACT

It's going to be awfully hard to host a party if you send out only half the invitations today, with the intention of mailing the other half tomorrow. Anyone who is in this mindset will inevitably forget to mail them or will be unsure of whether or not a certain invitation was sent.

Some things you'll need to do include the following:

1. **Call around.** Check the prices of competing businesses if you're planning on renting a limo, for example, or booking a hall. Don't assume that the price quote you get at one place is necessarily the going rate in your area.

2. **Don't be shy.** Businesses are accustomed to potential customers trying to keep their own costs down by comparing prices. Some businesses will try to accommodate your budget; others won't. Ask for their lowest rate. Take your business elsewhere if you can't work out a deal.

3. **Set a timetable for yourself.** If you're planning a bachelorette party during wedding and prom season and you want to hire a limo or a party bus, for example, you need to book these as early as possible. Don't wait till the week before the party, or you may be carrying around the guests piggyback.

4. **Be organized.** It bears repeating. Organization is the most important element to hosting a successful event.

Where Did I Put That?

Party planning involves so many details that your best plan of attack—and the best way to prevent major problems—is to get organized. Here are some helpful hints you should consider when it comes to getting organized:

- **Get a notebook.** Think of it as your party-planning diary. The guest list, important phone numbers, reminders to yourself of what needs to be paid when, ideas that pop into your head, notes of phone calls you've made and the names of your contacts—everything will be right there.
- **Get a filing system going.** Maybe you prefer color-coded folders. Maybe you like actual business files. Whatever your preference, set up a system and label everything. Give each area of planning its own separate file (menus, invitations, transportation, and so on). File everything in its appropriate place as needed.
- **The guest list.** Have a master list written in your notebook. As you fill out envelopes and stamp them, check names off this list. Keep this list handy so you can also check off RSVPs as they come in. Otherwise, you won't know who's coming and who isn't, even if you do remember to mail all the invitations.

- **Get everything in writing.** You don't want to find out the night of the bachelorette party that the restaurant employee you talked to was a flighty waitress who had no business booking a party of fifty in a room that seats thirty. Get all the confirmations in writing and keep all of these documents in the correct folder or file.

 ESSENTIAL

If you are extremely organized in your planning, you'll have much more leverage if you do encounter problems. Being able to pull out the contract you've signed or a receipt carries a lot more weight than your uncorroborated claims that you've already paid in full for the limo, for example.

Getting organized really isn't hard. Even the most hopeless clutter-lover can learn to put things where they belong. It's all in your attitude and the effort you're willing to make. The great thing is that if you can start out small—as in organizing your files for a party—the discipline may carry over into the rest of your life.

Reliable Guests

Bachelorette party guests have certain responsibilities, too. They aren't required to attend any function, nor are they obligated to send a gift if they can't make it to the party, but if they do accept an invitation, there are certain guidelines that they should abide by:

- **Attendance:** First of all, if you say you're going to be there, then be there. The hostess is planning food and drinks for a certain number of people.
- **On best behavior:** Even if the party is not to your taste, keep quiet. If you have a real problem with something, feel free to excuse yourself and leave, but don't ruin everyone else's fun.
- **Being realistic about expectations:** If you have a feeling you'll be uncomfortable riding around in a limo and ogling male dancers all night, stay home. Don't be pressured into attending a party that will make you squirm.

 QUESTION?

Do guests have to bring a gift to the bachelorette party?

The hostess should make it clear to the guests what type of gifts, if any, they are expected to bring. If you're planning on giving gag or risqué gifts, your guests will want to be in the know. This kind of information can also let the guests know what type of atmosphere you're planning and allow them to opt out of the party altogether if it's not their cup of tea.

Guests should remember that they were invited to the party and can't just take it over and steer it in the direction they want it to go in, even if they feel some things are inappropriate or too racy for their personal taste. This is, after all, a bachelorette party, and sometimes these parties are wild. Guests have no obligation to attend, but if they do, they should be courteous. If they're not enjoying themselves, they can leave. As the hostess, you have probably gone to a lot of trouble to honor the bride, and you shouldn't allow a cranky guest to be a party pooper. On the other hand, if you see that many of the guests are unhappy with the way the party is turning out, it may be helpful to steer a party in a different direction in order to accommodate them— especially if the bride-to-be is okay with that.

On Best Behavior

When guests call to RSVP, they should always ask the hostess if there's anything they could bring. As you know, a good rule of thumb is to never show up at any party empty-handed. Of course, if you absolutely and emphatically insist that your guests shouldn't bring a thing, they'll consider themselves in the clear.

You should also be able to rely on the guests to get the conversation going and keep everyone talking. One of the worst things that can happen to any party—aside from the roof collapsing—is for the conversation to fall flat. Although the bride and the hostess will probably be doing a lot of chitchatting, the rest of the guests should join in and help them out.

ESSENTIAL

Good guests are always looking to lend a helping hand if the situation arises. For example, you are having a heck of a time coordinating appetizers and keeping the bar stocked in your home. A guest could jump in there and help you serve the Brie or the fruit. However, keep in mind that guests are guests, and you can't expect them to spend the entire night cooking and cleaning in order to help you.

Realize that some people are shy, and that prevents them from starting a conversation with others. It's not that the groom's cousin hates you; she's probably intimidated by your grand vocabulary. (She heard you using the words *prenuptial agreement*.) Shyness can sometimes come off as snootiness, so make sure you don't confuse the two. You'll be surprised to find out that the quiet, uppity-looking coworker of the bride's has a killer sense of humor.

It's not only all right, but desirable to chat up strangers at a festive gathering like this. Strike up a conversation—go ahead and ask the groom's sister why she left her six-figure-salary job. Getting one conversation off the ground may work wonders for the atmosphere—conversation can spread like wildfire if the topics are right. Do your best and be a jovial guest.

Chapter 4

Start Making Decisions

When it comes to planning a bache-lorette party, you have lots of choices, and your only restrictions should be your budget and the expectations of the bride and the guests. You take it from there, and like a party magician, produce the best bachelorette party ever hosted. This chapter will cover some party-planning basics, as well as some specific bachelorette night reminders.

Scheduling the Event

One of the first decisions you need to make is the date of the event. Generally, bachelorette parties are hosted between two weeks and a month before the wedding day. Hosting the party the day before the wedding may sound like a good idea, but you don't want to send the bride staggering down the aisle with a hangover, and you certainly don't want her getting sick while she's attempting to say, "I do."

 FACT

> It's okay to ask the bride to choose a date that she's comfortable with for the bachelorette party. And the sooner you ask her, the better, especially if you're planning to host a large party that will require lots of preplanning.

Another reason you want to host the bachelorette well in advance of the wedding is because of time constraints. As the big day gets closer, the bride is going to have a million things to take care of, or at least it will seem that way to her. You know that if you throw her a party three weeks before the wedding, she won't *have* to be at the dressmaker's that day, all day—she still has time to fit her bachelorette party into her schedule.

You're Getting Married When?!

Not every bride has a long engagement. Some brides find Mr. Right and decide to become his Mrs.

within weeks. Sometimes wedding dates get moved up for one reason or another, such as in the event of something like a military deployment. Whatever the case, you have a short time to plan this particular bachelorette party, and you need to get moving.

What time of year it is will be a big factor in deciding how much you can actually do for the bride. For example: It's May, and she's getting married in three weeks. She wants a limo, a private room in a restaurant, and a block of rooms at the nicest hotel in town for an overnight party—all on a weekend night. You're going to have a very hard time fulfilling those requests. Late spring and summer are popular wedding, prom, and graduation seasons—people with prior notice of these events book limos, restaurants, and hotels months in advance.

That doesn't mean you shouldn't even bother checking things out. It just means you need to have an alternative party idea to present for the bride's approval.

 ALERT!

If you just can't find an opening anywhere, you'll have to go outside the original plan. Have the party at home, or go out to some clubs. You don't need reservations for these events, obviously, and you can throw together a great party in a short amount of time.

On the other hand, winter and fall months tend to be slower for restaurants, hotels, and limo companies. If it's January and she's tying the knot within weeks, you're probably going to find more options available.

What's Your Budget?

It's also important to consider how much money you want to spend on the party. Being able to spend more usually means less work for you, but you don't want to go broke for a night out with the girls, so be sure to consider your options. You have to decide which is more important to you in this case: Is it more important to keep costs down, or is it more important to save yourself some time and work?

Hosting a party at someone's house, for example, is obviously a lot cheaper than renting a room at the country club. However, a party at the club will involve a minimum effort from you in terms of cooking and cleaning—though you will, of course, end up paying for those services.

 ESSENTIAL

It may be worth the extra money to you to have the party somewhere else if you just can't see yourself serving dinner for twelve— or appetizers for fifty. As long as you can reasonably afford it, there's no reason you shouldn't take the party somewhere else.

Be realistic about what you're willing and able to do, both financially and physically. First things first: Don't invite a slew of people over for a bachelorette dinner if you're paying for everything, you can't cook, and you're broke. This is an equation for disaster. Either you'll go into debt paying for this party, or people will arrive hungry and be served cheese and crackers with water.

Parties at Home

This is one of the cheapest ways to go. There's no rental cost, and you can plan any menu that fits your budget. You have the most flexibility in planning a party at home—it can be as small or as large as you want, with whatever kind of entertainment you want, with whatever kind of food you want. No one's going to sock you with a bill for unexpected expenses, such as gratuities or "restocking fees." You know what you're spending if you're keeping close track of expenses.

You may be planning on inviting very few guests or as many as you can pack into your place. The biggest consideration is that you're going to be responsible for food, drinks, and entertainment. This can be a daunting task if you've never hosted a party. Here are some ways to make it easier on yourself:

- **Determine your budget.** There's no sense in moving forward until you decide on how large and extravagant a party you can afford.
- **Decide on the number of guests.** This will determine your menu (i.e., appetizers for fifty or dinner

for six) and the feel of your party. A small guest list will lend itself to an intimate gathering, of course, while a large list will result in more mingling.

- **Plan a menu.** Decide if you're serving light fare or something more substantial. (Serving nothing at all is not an option.) And make sure you let your guests know what they can expect when they arrive. If you're making a big dinner, you want the guests to arrive hungry.

- **Don't forget the drinks.** Since bachelorette parties tend to be a time of celebration and imbibing, stock your bar well. (Don't forget swizzle sticks and fruit.) Have some soda and juice on hand as well for any guests who don't drink alcohol.

- **Consider your options for entertainment.** Are you going to play games? Will there be gifts? Have you arranged for a stripper? Consider how raucous the bachelorette party is going to be and plan accordingly.

- **Enlist some help.** Not everyone is a natural-born party giver. If you're screaming, "I can't do this!" ask a friend or two to help out with the food, for example, and *acknowledge their assistance,* both privately and by letting the guests know that you weren't the one who made the outstanding clam dip.

Getting Out

If you just don't want to bother with the cooking and cleaning that accompany a party at home, or if you're planning a bachelorette party out of town, there are plenty of options available to you. Some brides enjoy a small bachelorette dinner at a nice restaurant. You can always arrange for a bigger party at a banquet hall or rent out a restaurant room if the bride has a large family or many friends she wants to include.

 FACT

A party that includes the cost of renting a room somewhere and having a caterer or restaurant prepare the food and drinks is likely to cost substantially more than a party at home. This is the type of party that may require you to sign on an extra hostess or two to defray costs.

If you're planning a party in a nice restaurant, make sure to check with the management as to what they will and will not allow in the form of entertainment. While most facilities will not object to tasteful gift-giving, some will put the kibosh on adult toys being passed around during their peak dinner hours. Also, a party in a respectable establishment may nix any plans you have for hiring an exotic male dancer to delight your guests.

If you are having a party in a place where other groups of people will be present, be considerate of the fact that they are also paying customers. You do not have the right to be unreservedly obnoxious just because your friend is getting married. If that's your plan, have a party at home, where you can get as wild as you want—or as wild as your neighbors will allow.

Another perk of having a sit-down dinner in a restaurant is that most guests will expect to pay for their own meal. If a Dutch treat is your plan, make it clear to the invited guests beforehand. You should still offer to pick up the desert and bar bill if you want to be a hostess and not just a shepherd. It's an extra-nice touch.

Mix and Match

You can also create a hybrid of these two settings. You want the party at home, but you don't want to cook and serve and be bothered with table linens and washing dishes? Who does, really? Hire a caterer to take care of all these things. The price of this luxury can include setup, food, service, and cleanup. Different caterers offer different services, depending on the size of their organization and their specialties. (A catering service that's run from a restaurant will offer more choices than your neighbor who prepares everything in her small kitchen.)

Many organizations can only offer "drop off" service; they'll make the food and bring it over, but you'll have to do the rest. Some will allow you to purchase appetizers alone. Some offer full-course meals. Make some calls and do some research in your area. If you're splitting the bill several ways for this party, the price may well be worth it to all of you—and you know you won't get stuck doing all the dirty work alone at the end of the night.

 QUESTION?

Do I need to tip the caterer?
Generally speaking, no. Gratuities are usually added to the bill if a server is involved—but check your contract and make sure.

It's Time to Be Spontaneous

There are parties at home and parties in restaurants. But maybe the bride is looking for a little more action, something a little more unpredictable. Use your creative instincts. Many women opt for something a little different for their bachelorette parties. Sometimes this actually requires less planning than having everyone over to your house or meeting everyone at a set time.

During a less structured evening, the setting takes center stage and the partiers become participants in it. As long as no one in the group needs to be checking off items on a timetable ("All right, it's ten-thirty. We've tangoed with some Spanish-speaking men, next we'll be doing belly-button shots on the bar, which will put us at eleven fifteen, when we need to enter the wet T-shirt contest . . ."), this kind of impulsiveness can be a lot of fun. You don't know exactly what the evening has in store for you, but it's going to be a little crazy.

The Portable Party

Many bachelorette parties take place all around town, in club after club, all night long. If this type of party is right up your alley, consider hiring a limo or a party bus. You'll be able to shake your booty till the sun comes up, and you'll arrive home safely, which is the most important thing. Another perk here is that your circle of party people can grow by leaps and bounds, if you want it to.

The cost of transportation can be split between the guests, but, again, make it very clear before the party that everyone will be expected to pony up a certain amount. Don't count the bride as a guest—you should all pitch in to pay her way.

 ESSENTIAL

Be sure to book your transportation early enough. Prime wedding seasons (spring and summer) coincide with many graduations and proms, whose participants will also be looking for a chauffeur.

Male Dance Clubs

Ah, muscular men baring it (almost) all in the name of entertaining wild women. This is the image that most often comes to mind upon hearing the words *bachelorette party*. Lots of bachelorette groups like to visit these establishments and let loose their primal screams. Whether you want to make an entire evening of it is up to the bride. Some women really enjoy watching writhing, oiled men dance till they drop. Other women feel that—in this particular situation—less is more.

These dance clubs have become something of a rite of passage for many brides, so you may want to include at least a brief visit on your list of things to do on Bachelorette Night. Who knows? Maybe you girls will be the last ones dragged out by the bouncers at the end of the night, still yelling for more. Don't forget to bring plenty of crisp bills. You know why.

Ahoy, Sailor!

If you're fortunate enough to live in an area full of waterfront clubs and restaurants, charter a boat to float you and the girls up and down the waterway. Not only will you have your transportation taken care of, you'll have a floating party going on. This is not the best idea if anyone in your group has motion sickness, of course.

Another idea to accommodate the bride who just loves the water is to have a dinner cruise bachelorette party. There are some beautiful ships that will drift you all over the harbor—or lake, or canal—while you and the girls enjoy a lovely bachelorette dinner. Check around in your area to see what's available. (For obvious reasons, many of these dinner cruises are seasonal in some regions.)

Room Service!

If you and the girls are coming from every end of the city to celebrate the bachelorette party, consider reserving a few rooms in a nice hotel. You girls can party to your hearts' content and you won't have to worry about getting home safely. You'll just have to manage to remember which room is yours, which can be difficult enough when you're sober. More information on planning your party in a hotel, and all over town, is included in Chapter 9.

From Rowdy to Subdued

You should choose your party place based on your guests and what you expect to do with them. Are your guests big partiers? Are older women (who are presumably a little more reserved) going to be in attendance? Is this a daytime party, an after-work gathering, or an all-nighter?

 ALERT!

> Don't try to plan a party where you're going to hit all the hot clubs in town all night and then invite the bride's very conservative Aunt Betty to ride along in the limo. She won't come, and she may be insulted by the fact that you invited her at all to an evening she wouldn't even consider. Scale back your party or your guest list.

The Wild Bunch

Your guest list is full of women who like to have a good time—a *really* good time. What to do with them? First, realize that anything you do will likely turn into a frenzy, so plan accordingly. This isn't the group to take to a small, crowded restaurant. They will clear the place as soon as the drinks start flowing.

With a group like this, you have to decide how much of the evening you want to orchestrate and how much you want to leave to fate. The best part of hosting a gathering with a group like this is that you don't have to plan every little detail, like where everyone's going to sit, and what sort of centerpieces to use, because these women don't care. They're simply out for a good time.

The biggest decision to be made is whether you're going to keep these ladies under wraps at home or spring them on the town. Bear in mind that inviting a rambunctious group to your home seems like a good idea at 7 P.M., but it starts to lose its luster by about 3 A.M., especially if you are an apartment dweller with tired and irate neighbors who prefer sleeping at that hour.

The good news is that it's very likely that a wild bunch like this wants to see and be seen, so you may be off the hook as far as keeping them under control. Put a group like this in their natural environment: a bar, a dance club, or any other place resembling a human zoo.

QUESTION?

Is the hostess responsible for paying all the expenses for a wild night out on the town?
You're in luck. Often, the cost can be amicably shared between the guests. For example, if you're planning on spending the evening barhopping, you can all take turns paying for rounds of drinks, or run a tab and split it at evening's end.

Toning Things Down

The word *bachelorette* carries with it a connotation of wild behavior and out-of-control women. This isn't always the case. There's absolutely no reason why you can't host a respectful, clean gathering and still call it a bachelorette party. After all, this is a party to honor the bride. There's no by-law of etiquette that states there has to be a fountain of vodka for your guests to bathe in.

If you've been agonizing over the guest list because the bride really wants to include her whole family—including her very stern sister—stop your self-torture now. Remember, this is a party for the bride and you're supposed to respect what she wants. Disregarding her feelings or the feelings of some of the guests, like the serious-minded sister, will cause more problems than you want to take on. The bride doesn't want her guests to be uncomfortable. She doesn't want to have to apologize or offer explanations for anything in the wake of her bachelorette party, least of all her friendship with you. Keep that in mind and plan accordingly.

A mellower version of the bachelorette party is definitely a possibility. Opt to host a luncheon, for example, or make it more of a picnic setting. The bride will be getting a chance to attend one more event in her honor before her wedding, and you'll come out the champ for keeping things in control.

A Mixed Bunch

If you are trying to mix groups—for example, you have some wild guests and some subdued guests invited to the same event, with the intent of keeping things mellow—you, as the hostess, are responsible for keeping things under control. This (unfortunately) includes taking responsibility for any guest who gets outrageously drunk and starts dancing in a suggestive manner in full view of the bride's grandmother.

 ALERT!

Clear lines of communication are key. If it's at all appropriate, mention to the potentially objectionable guests that this is going to be a squeaky-clean event. If a prior consultation is just not possible, then you need to deal with it as it happens. Think of yourself not only as the hostess, but also as the censorship committee for this party.

One way to avoid this potential problem, if you sense it will *be* a problem, is to have an alcohol-free party. It may be a party pooper for some guests, but you will breathe easier if you know you have nixed the proverbial fuel that adds to their fire.

Making It a Girls' Weekend

Maybe you and the bride are part of a tight-knit group from college that has dispersed across the country since graduation. Maybe the bride and her sister and cousins just don't get together like they used to. A fun alternative to a single-evening event is turning the bachelorette party into an entire weekend of events. Not only will the bride get to see everyone, you'll all have the chance to really catch up with one another and not feel pressured into fitting all your conversations into one night.

When it comes to getting away for a weekend with the girls, there are many options to choose from. Here are a few ideas:

- **Book some rooms at a spa.** You'll be able to take full advantage of their offerings, from facials to massages to mud baths.
- **Get outdoors.** If the bride and her friends are outdoor nuts, take the party to Mother Nature. Go skiing. Book a campsite. Climb a mountain. Go skydiving. You'll feel you've earned your evenings sitting around doing nothing but chatting.
- **Open your home.** Nothing is more fun than having

a group of girlfriends to your home for the weekend. Since you know the area, you can let them in on the great little boutiques down on Main Street, and the excellent cafés where all of you can rest your tired feet after cleaning out the shops.

Obviously, some of these destinations will be more costly than others and if you're all planning on going to a hotel for the weekend, for example, you'll be more of an organizer than a hostess. The good news is that if you're into the idea of getting away for the weekend, it can be done on a shoestring budget. It's a matter of setting your priorities and sticking with them.

 FACT

Considering that the cost of some getaways can seem pretty steep for some women, you can always present it as a group bachelorette/wedding gift for the bride. Think of it as the gift that everyone can enjoy.

A Relaxing Getaway

The bachelorette weekend doesn't necessarily have to be an extravagant affair. For example, Becky was planning a bachelorette party for her best friend, Alex. Becky's parents own a modest home on a lake in New England, and they allowed Becky to invite the bachelorette group up to the house for the weekend. Says

Becky: "It was just such a mellow weekend. We had a group of eight and we slept wherever we could find room. No one felt the need to get stinking drunk before midnight. We went into town and had dinner at this quiet little place one night, and we ordered in the other night. Alex loved it and really felt like she touched base with her closest girlfriends over the course of two days instead of in a few hours. This was four years ago, and we still all talk about what a great weekend that was."

You can, of course, go all-out and plan a weekend in paradise, like Maggie, who had her bachelorette party at an all-inclusive resort in the Caribbean. Everyone paid her own way and chipped in on paying for Maggie as well. Says Maggie: "What a great way to really relax before the whole wedding swung into full gear. My husband and I weren't planning a honeymoon until six months after our wedding—the first opportunity he had to take vacation time from work—so this was a much-needed pre-wedding getaway for me."

The group of six women booked a long weekend at a beach-front resort, soaked up the rays, took advantage of the swim-up bar in the pool, and learned what a Mocko Jumbie is. Were they exhausted at the end of the weekend? Sure. Would they do it again for another friend's bachelorette party? "In a second," Maggie says.

Pick Your Escapade

Another idea that's gaining popularity as brides wait longer to get married—and they and their friends have more money at their disposal—is to hit the casinos in

Las Vegas. You can try your luck at the blackjack tables, see a show, browse in the boutiques, and ride a roller coaster all in one day. (Don't plan on sleeping. That's not part of *this* trip.)

If cost is just a small consideration for you and the girls, the possibilities for this type of bachelorette party are endless. Check out New York. Or go rustic. Hasn't the bride always wanted to go to a dude (or is that dudette) ranch? You want to make sure, of course, that these plans don't overlap with her honeymoon plans, so get together with her, pick a place, and go!

 ALERT!

If these potential problems are giving you a potential headache, it may be best to keep your guest list for the getaway as limited as possible. This is not the best time for the bride to get better acquainted with her office mates. Know who's coming, and know them well.

No matter where you're off to, don't forget to load up on the souvenirs. This trip is commemorating the bride's last days as a single woman. Pick up something that will remind her of her last voyage as a maiden. You can choose something typically touristy and tacky, or choose something a little nicer that she can actually display in her new home—a piece of pottery or a nice picture frame.

Selective Invitations

A couple of words of caution about a Bachelorette Girls' Weekend: First, keep in mind that *vacation* isn't synonymous with *perfection*. Just because you're all getting together to toast your engaged friend, it doesn't necessarily mean that personalities will suddenly be transformed. Vacations tend to bring out the best or the worst in people.

If the bride has two friends who are constantly at each other's throats, and both are included in her bachelorette getaway, bring along that supersized bottle of ibuprofen. Any adversaries may well annoy each other even *more* on vacation, especially when both realize that they've just dropped a whole lot of money—or at least a few days' time—to vacation with a person they despise. You may see them jockeying for the bride's attention or they may show the same nastiness they would display toward one another if they were back home.

Secondly, match the weekend guest list to your expected activities. It's going to be difficult to spend a weekend skiing side-by-side with the bride, and more difficult to catch her attention for those fireside chats if the guest list reads like a phone book.

Also, keep in mind that weekends and getaways like these are much more likely to go smoothly if the guests are close to the bride. An exception to this may include inviting members of the groom's immediate family—and even that is a risky proposition if they're little more than strangers to the bride. You're going away for a few days.

If things are going badly (for example, the groom's sister just cannot believe how much you all drink and smoke and swear), there's very little relief in sight. You're stuck.

 ESSENTIAL

> The entire point of a bachelorette party weekend is to have a fun time. Unlike a comparatively brief party at home, you will be spending *days* with these people—days that will seem like months, or years, or decades, if any major personality disorders should pop up among the guests.

Out on a Weeknight

You have a situation: The bride is just too darn busy to come to her own bachelorette party on a weekend night. She's booked solid with work, or dress fittings, or meetings with caterers every weekend for about the next six months. Or maybe it's that her fiancé is out of town, and she can't bear to go a couple of weeks without seeing him, even though it means nixing bachelorette plans.

Wait just a minute there. You're not using your noggin. Who says this party has to be on a weekend? Why not have her party during the week? It may not be the wild bachelorette bash you imagined you'd be hosting for your friend, but remember—the whole point of the party is to toast the bride one last time before the wedding. You can do that any night of the week.

 ALERT!

> If you're planning on hiring a stripper, have him arrive at a decent hour. Don't make your guests hang around till midnight just so they feel like they didn't miss the main event. Or worse, they might all leave, and you'll be left all alone with a muscular man who's wearing rip-away clothes.

A party on a weeknight is likely to be shorter and mellower than a weekend party, due to the simple fact that just about everyone will have to be up for work the next morning. Plan accordingly. Not everyone will want to play drinking games on a Tuesday night. Center your activities around chitchat and food. Have some games and activities planned that will keep people talking and having a good time. Also make sure you stock plenty of nonalcoholic drinks.

Chapter 5

Work Out the Details

You've been to big parties. You've been to small parties. Perhaps you've even attended a coed bachelor/bachelorette party. As you try to narrow down all of your options and begin working out the details, you may need some help along the way—and this chapter is here to serve as your guide.

Let's Review the Bride's Agenda

So, do you know what the bride is thinking? Finding out is a tall order as far as some brides are concerned, but it's a necessary chore. Think of it as an amateur analysis of your friend. If she says she wants an intimate gathering, but the first draft of the guest list includes everyone she's ever met, what's the explanation? If she says she wants a huge party, but she honestly doesn't know that many people, what does that mean? Does she want all of her guests to bring a friend? Does she feel that small parties are no fun?

 ESSENTIAL

You need to get into the bride's mind and find out what's going on in there. If she's feeling guilty about not inviting the cousin of the girl she used to work with—and she was a distant relation at that—she may be going overboard just a bit. She may end up with a party full of strangers who really couldn't care less about her or her upcoming wedding.

You need to get to the bottom of this. It sounds simple and a little silly, but this is the base from which you're moving to plan the entire party. In the case of the bride who's inviting friends of friends of friends, ask her directly—does she want a small party or not? What kind of atmosphere is she thinking of? Does she feel like she has to invite people so that no one will be offended?

In the case of the other type of bride, ask her—does she mind that her bachelorette party will be full of strangers? Some brides really won't mind, and live by that old adage, "The more, the merrier."

Small Parties Are Intimate

This party may be a walk in the park for you if the bride simply wants to invite the tight little group you've both been a part of since you were ten. If, on the other hand, you're hosting a small bachelorette party with the idea of introducing the bride's friends to the groom's family, you've got your work cut out for you.

A small affair is definitely the best way to get people together with the idea of knowing each other well at evening's end. Your guests will pretty much be forced to sit and talk to one another. It's also easier, as the hostess, to initiate conversation that's interesting or pertinent to everyone.

The less attractive side of a small party is that if things are going badly, they tend to go *very* badly—and quick. It's hard to salvage a gathering where the guests have no desire to speak to one another, for example.

Be Prepared

There are several ways to make your small bachelorette party run a little more smoothly. Have your topics of conversation ready. Know a little bit about your guests. Asking someone about her unusual line of work (the bride's sister makes artificial hearts) or something interesting in her life (the groom's cousin was stuck in that huge hurricane in the Caribbean) is an automatic conversation starter.

Keep the party machine oiled. Nothing kills an already faltering party faster than running out of appetizers or wine. Have everything you need at the ready, and keep replenishing your supplies.

Background music conceals the fact that the conversation sounds like a revving engine—it's trying to get going, but it's falling flat, at least in the party's opening moments. Once the guests get fueled up with food and drink, things will run more smoothly.

 ALERT!

> Anticipation is your ace in the hole. Without being a complete pessimist, try to imagine the worst that can happen—and plan for it. For example, what will you do if you run out of dip? The key is to prepare in advance.

Big-Party Basics

Big parties are big on fun. While they can be a lot of work to plan and pull off successfully, they can also be a tour de force—parties like this often take off simply because of the volume of guests, and once the party gets moving, there's no stopping it.

If you have very little party-planning experience under your belt, the thought of hosting a big event may send chills down your spine. Don't think that you have to start small just because you're new to the hostess scene. A little planning goes a long way, and a little help goes even further—so read on!

 ESSENTIAL

If you're having the bachelorette party in a restaurant or bar—anywhere you're not directly responsible for feeding and watering the guests—you're not completely excused from your duties as hostess. You still need to look out for the other guests. They made the effort to come to this party; show them a good time.

You Don't Have to Go It Alone

The first thing to recognize is that you may need some assistance. Think of this as a mathematical equation, like throwing a small party—times three, or five, or eight, depending on how large your guest list is. Everything will be done on a bigger scale. You'll need more room, more food, more drinks—more everything.

Although it's easy enough to estimate the raw materials you'll need for a bigger get-together, putting it all together is another story. Do you really want to be solely responsible for stuffing all those mushrooms—not to mention preparing the rest of the food—in addition to decorating, seeing to entertainment, cleaning up after your guests, and playing bartender?

There's no shame in asking for help. No one's going to think any less of you. The most experienced party giver will still need help with basic logistics. She'll have someone take coats while she's putting out appetizers. Or she'll have someone keep an eye on the ice supply while she puts the finishing touches on the cake. You can't be in two places at once. It's that simple.

QUESTION?

Do I really have to baby-sit my guests? They're adults, for goodness' sake.
Looking out for the guests and making sure they're having a good time isn't baby-sitting—in fact, it's one of your duties as a hostess. If you see someone who looks completely uncomfortable, draw her into the conversation. Get her situated with a group before you get back to the kitchen, or bar, or dance floor.

Get Things Shaking

The next step is getting a big party off and running. Plan some sort of entertainment—funky music and dancing, if the notion grabs you, and/or the all-important male stripper. If you're hosting this bachelorette party at home, leave your post in the kitchen when you have a minute to check on food and drink supplies, or ask someone at the party to keep an eye on them for you. You'll also want to make sure that your guests are mingling and the party is heading in the right direction.

One great thing about hosting a larger bachelorette party is that conversation will usually take care of itself, as long as you ply everyone with enough food and drink. After all, the bride's friends are coming together to toast her and have a good time.

Going Coed

It's a new millennium. People disregard the rules of party giving all the time in search of new, better, or just more convenient standards. One such standard is that a bachelorette party is a women-only affair. If you want to challenge the convention, consider the following:

- Are some of the bride's best friends men?
- Does the bride-to-be in your life just have to be with her man every single minute?
- Is the entire wedding party a tight-knit clan from high school or college, and having separate parties just seems too formal and a waste of time?
- Could you pick the Best Man out of a lineup, or is his identity a complete mystery to you, even though you're the Maid of Honor?

If these situations are ringing a bell with you, you may want to think about hosting a coed bachelor/bachelorette party for the bride and groom.

The Bride Is One of the Guys

Some women have very close ties with their male friends. In fact, a man can be the best friend a girl can have, especially if he is also a friend of the groom. Take Lindsay, for instance, who is engaged to Pete. They've dated for five years, and for the majority of that time, Pete has been in the service, which has left Lindsay at home and missing him. But she hasn't been alone. When Pete's friends saw how completely devastated Lindsay was after her boyfriend left, they stepped in and became the big brothers she never had.

 FACT

Let's say the bride works with more men than women, and everyone in the office (or restaurant, or garage) gets along famously. Or she's coming out of college and her sorority has worked hand-in-hand with the fraternity down the street, raising money for charities and throwing the occasional toga party. Both are good reasons to host a coed party.

Says Lindsay: "It may sound really old-fashioned, but this group of guys really watches out for me. I work in the same building as Jack, for example, and if I have to stay late for a meeting or to get some filing work done, he usually waits for me and walks me to my car. I really feel like these guys are some of the best friends I could ever have. They cheer me up when I miss Pete, and we hang out at the pub down the street together. There's no question that they treat me like a sister, and it's awesome."

Lindsay cannot imagine having a bachelorette party without these guys, and because they're also Pete's friends, it would be really silly to have two parties and invite the same people.

A Family Affair

Perhaps the bride's family is a sprawling but tight-knit group, and she can't imagine having a crazy bachelorette party without her male cousins present. Mary is part of such a clan: "My brothers and my cousins are my family and my best friends. I'm one of only three girls in the entire family. We were all raised on the same block, and have always just genuinely loved being around one another. They're all so happy for me, and they really like my fiancé, but they definitely don't want to go to a bachelor party that they feel may be disrespectful toward me. We're doing a coed party for that reason, and because my fiancé has four sisters who really want to honor him."

Guarding Her Groom

Your engaged friend is so in love with her man that she cannot imagine having her bachelorette party without him, she says. You suspect she's actually so worried about what might happen at his bachelor party that she doesn't want him out of her sight. Don't question her motives. Be supportive and nonjudgmental. Remember that many grooms are caught up in what their *friends* want out of a bachelor party—something the bride doesn't have to worry about since you're the ideal friend and hostess with excellent listening skills.

Also keep in mind that not every groom necessarily wants a wild bachelor party. Some men would rather spend the evening with their sweetie and a group of friends than in the bosom of an exotic dancer. Since his male friends may be less supportive of a quiet evening than the bride's friends, a coed party gives the groom a perfect out. This is the combined sendoff for the lovebirds. End of story.

Meet Me in the Middle

If there's some disagreement over whether the party should be coed, a good way to compromise is to have two separate parties that join up at a certain point during the night. Everyone will be having a great time by that point, so pick an appropriate place (one that will still be jumping at that hour) and continue your good times together. This way the bride and groom can go home together and not have to question each other about how they ended their evenings.

Who's My Partner?

Another reason to consider a coed party is if the two sides of the wedding party need a chance to meet. Marcy, a bridesmaid in her friend Karen's wedding, cohosted a coed party at her home. "I was really relieved to meet the guys in the wedding a month before the actual event," she says. "The bridesmaids and the groomsmen came from two completely different areas of the city we live in, and the two groups didn't know each other at all. We had a group of about twenty, and we spent the whole night just having fun and getting to know each other without the stress of knowing the wedding was the next day, like we would have felt if we had met at the rehearsal dinner.

 ALERT!

Don't use a coed party as a matchmaking adventure. No one falls for this, and you're risking resentful and embarrassed guests if they feel they're being forced into making small talk with a stranger of your choosing. If two guests feel comfortable with each other and hit it off by chance, sit back and be happy your party is a success.

"It was a low-key party—no strippers, no games, just a night to celebrate Karen and Bill's engagement and marriage. When we all did meet up again at the rehearsal dinner, it was like running into old friends. The wedding day itself went really smoothly, and I think it was because the entire wedding party had spent a good chunk of time together beforehand."

Karen, the bride, was equally relieved: "This could have been a disaster. Bill's friends are very different from my friends, and I honestly couldn't see how they were going to get along and mingle on the day of the wedding. I had visions of a junior high dance, with the groomsmen on one side of the dance floor totally ignoring the bridesmaids. Having this party was the perfect thing to bring everyone together in a relaxed atmosphere just to meet each other. It worked out so well, I would advise anyone in the same position to do the same thing."

Chances are, you'll want to host this type of party at a locale where mingling is easy, so that everyone can talk and feel at ease. This is the type of party to have at home or at the small, uncrowded bar your family owns. You want to avoid extra-loud, jam-packed places like dance clubs. You can't really get to know the groom's brother if you're yelling over the techno-beat and getting jostled around by people getting their grooves on.

Division of Labor

If you do decide on hosting a joint bachelor/bachelorette party, and you're thinking of something more formal than meeting in a tavern and spreading the news via word-of-mouth, it's a good idea to find a cohost. If you're wondering why, consider the following reasons:

- Any party that includes two separate sets of friends and/or relatives is probably going to be larger and more expensive than a single-gender gathering.
- Because this is a party that will bring the groom's friends together with the bride's friends, the groups' expectations may be very different. You may want caviar, and the groom's friends may want frank-furters. It's good to have both points of view repre-sented by the two cohosts.
- You want to toast the newlyweds; the groom's friends want to toast them, too. Working together on this will not only impress your engaged friends, it will genuinely make them happy to see their two worlds merging successfully.

 ESSENTIAL

As with any cohosting situation, you're going to work *with* someone. Remember "compro-mise"? If you know you're a little bossy, be extra careful. If the men are determined to bring a beer ball to this bash, feel free to bring a classy wine. Work it out. Don't make your engaged friends find a new wedding party at this point.

Making Your Case

An ideal cohosting gig would go something like this: You've spoken with the bride and groom, who have both expressed their wishes to hold a combined bachelor/bachelorette party. You take the reins for the girls' effort and contact the most obvious groomsman—let's say it's the groom's brother or his best friend. Assuming the two of you have never laid eyes on each other, this can be an awkward undertaking for a meek bridesmaid, but it's a necessary step. You can do it. If you need a little advice, ask the bride who would be the best option for a cohost. She may have a more objective opinion of her fiancé's friends and would know which of them are responsible enough to work with you.

Hopefully, when you do make contact, this idea won't be hitting the groom's buddy out of the blue, but as men are generally less communicative with each other than women are with their friends, it may be that this is the first he's hearing about a coed party. No sweat.

Your job is to successfully impart to him the pros of having such a party, including the significant fact that the groom wants it. You want to be friendly, businesslike, and have a few ideas at the ready—but you do *not* want to be bossy.

Hopefully, the groomsman agrees to be your cohost, but what does that mean? Some men will want to take an active part in the planning. Others will acknowledge that they don't know what's appropriate for a coed party and leave it in your hands.

Agreeing on the Atmosphere

You both need to be open and honest about your respective expectations. For example, is he expecting to hire a bevy of belly dancers and have them drop in at your house? Are you planning the same thing, although the groomsmen may be less than comfortable with a male stripper in their midst? Is he thinking chips and salsa, and you're thinking catered affair? And what about expenses? If he's thinking the groom's side is willing to contribute $30 and you're thinking more like $300, hard feelings are in your future.

Assuming you can find some kind of middle ground, you've got your green light to go ahead and start planning. If, on the other hand, this groomsman is someone you clash with or someone you just feel you don't trust, scrap the cohosting plans.

 ALERT!

It's better to take matters into your own hands than to be stuck with a bunch of bills by a dishonest friend of the groom. Not only will you end up holding the bag, but the goodwill this party should foster will end up dead in its tracks as well. Resentment will be the theme of the party, and there will be no hiding it from the bride and groom.

In the event that this does happen, don't fret too much. Do what you can on your own, and forget the visions of grandeur. Explain to the bride that it may not be possible to have the exact type of party she wanted, but don't badmouth the groomsman in question. She has enough on her mind without refereeing a fight between you and her groom's pal.

Chapter 6

Put Together the Guest List

Now, it's time to start drawing up your guest list, and there are several things you must consider. Most importantly, the guests you choose to invite should reflect the bride's idea of what her bachelorette party should be like. If she's got a penchant for partying, make sure that the guests you invite won't be offended by any overtly risqué goings-on—and vice versa.

It Depends on the Bride

The bride is the starting point for this party. For instance, if you know that she's not a big drinker, you shouldn't bother organizing a drunken bachelorette bash for her. If, on the other hand, you know that the bride is looking forward to a few drinks with the girls, you'd better provide the opportunity to get those drinks.

 ESSENTIAL

> Just because the bride doesn't imbibe doesn't mean she doesn't know how to have fun. She may still enjoy the strip clubs and the limo, the naughty games and the scavenger hunts. Some of the goofiest and most fun-loving women out there never touch alcohol, and they absolutely know how to have a great time without it.

Similarly, you have to consider how the bride's attitude toward drinking will affect the guest list. If the bride is a teetotaler, she probably expects most of her guests to follow suit. While most women understand and accept a friend or acquaintance's nonalcoholic preferences, it would be more in keeping with the spirit of the party if most guests would join the bride in downing those Cosmopolitans. On the other hand, if the bride doesn't drink, she may not like it if her guests aren't willing to give up their cocktails for an evening of fun without the liquor.

Networking and Bachelorette Parties

In addition to making sure that the guests match the type of party you have in mind, there are several other factors to consider as well. As you put together the guest list, keep in mind that there are some people who will be best kept off it.

Here's one example. You know the bride is a big old partier. She can drink anyone you know under the table, and she is *so* looking forward to her bachelorette party. You're a little worried that she wants to invite her entire office—and rightly so. There are some guests that need to be whittled away right from the get-go—not because of anything *they've* done, but because it's in the bride's best interest. These are guests who do not necessarily know that the bride has a heart of gold. They don't have to forgive her behavior (like her family does)—and they won't.

While most parties are fair game for making contacts and increasing goodwill between coworkers, bachelorette parties should be taken off the list. There is just no possibility that the bride's boss is going to be impressed with the bride's ability to do a shot without using her hands. Ask anyone who has ever made a spectacle of themselves at an office holiday party—office politics and alcohol-laden parties do not mix.

Avoid Negative Consequences

In a situation like this, it often happens that someone will end up feeling very uncomfortable—and woe to the bride if it's her boss. Sure, the bride should cut loose at her bachelorette party, but for that very reason, her boss should not be in attendance.

Remember, life goes on after the bachelorette party. You should assume that the bride will want to have her job and her business contacts come Monday morning. Implore her, beg her, do anything you can to convince her that inviting business contacts to her bachelorette party is probably not a good idea.

 ALERT!

> It's a good idea to discuss the number of guests with the bride. Although this is her party, you should be comfortable with the size of the event that you're about to host. Avoid making too many last-minute additions, which may throw off your preparations.

Old Friends and the New Crew

The bride has a life she left behind: Say for instance, she's from a rural area and moved to the big city some years back. Her former life looks nothing like her current one—and her old friends, from what you hear about them, are very different from the crew the bride surrounds herself with these days. Perhaps the bride left that life behind because she wanted something new, but her wedding has made her nostalgic for her childhood buddies.

There's nothing wrong with two groups of different women getting together to celebrate a mutual friend's good fortune. Sometimes these meetings go much better than you could have anticipated—but sometimes they are far worse than you ever dreamed they could be.

This is your friend's bachelorette party. It's supposed to be a fun night for everyone. If you suspect that the two groups of friends are never going to mix, speak up before you send out invitations. It's a lot easier to make the bride understand your point of view (and chances are she will—she's the one with the new life, remember) than to try to mingle with strangers who are eyeing you up suspiciously, thinking you stole their old friend from them.

Perfect Strangers

Is the bride the type of woman who makes new friends every day? She joins a new gym, she has a new pal. She gets coffee at the new coffee shop, she has another new pal. She's outside putting change in the meter, and she comes back to the office to tell you about the great meter maid she just met—her newest pal.

Women who are superfriendly are a rare breed in this busy world where most people don't have time to look at one another; while this may be a great personality trait and something the bride truly enjoys, you need to let her know that the guest list cannot grow by two or three women every day, depending on whom she happens to be chatting with on the subway or at the bank. Inviting perfect strangers by the dozen just isn't fair to you, and it's going to make for an awkward gathering if most of the guests are strangers to one another.

When Mom's Invited

The bride is extremely close to her mother and wouldn't dream of having an event without her. This is great news if the mother of the bride happens to be Goldie Hawn or Sharon Osbourne. For everyone else, though, this situation will greatly affect the planning of the bachelorette party. If the bride's conservative mother will be in attendance, you can't host a wild night of shenanigans and expect her to think it was a terrific evening.

 FACT

> Many bachelorette parties include only close friends of the bride, because they end up being rowdy, randy events that would make the bride's mom blush. However, having the bride's mother or other relatives there is perfectly acceptable as well.

Your first line of defense is a heart-to-heart chat with the bride. You need to get a feel for whom she wants at her party, and the type of party she wants. For the sake of argument, let's say she wants a party brimming with drinks and boogying all night long, but she also wants her great aunt there. Are these two requests really compatible?

Another issue you'll have to deal with is whether the aunt will be offended if she's not included in every single pre-wedding event. Some families are so close that they do everything together, and excluding a member is a huge insult. On the other hand, some older women may be offended to be invited to a wild affair. Tread lightly and listen to the bride. Hopefully, she has enough common sense to lead you down the right trail.

Is Mom In?

If the bride insists on having her mom or older female relatives in attendance, you need to assess the situation. Remember, as a hostess, this party will reflect on you. Do you want Mrs. Mother of the Bride—whom you've known since childhood and who has always thought of you as a decent girl—to attend a party you're giving where there will be adult toys and trashy lingerie given as gifts to her daughter?

If her mom is a randy sort herself, problem solved. If she is not, you'll have a lot of explaining to do, as well as all those awkward postparty glances to deal with for years to come. Not to mention that what is done in good fun at a bachelorette party can some-times be twisted in the hands of an angry and/or embarrassed party-going mom and will come out sounding like it was a depraved event to those who weren't there.

ALERT!

If there's even the slightest chance that the bride's mom will be insulted by not receiving an invitation, open up your lines of communication. While going into as little detail as possible, explain to her that this party may not be her cup of tea, but that she is welcome to attend.

In the end, there's very little you can do in the event that the bride wants a wild party and her mom in attendance, too. You have to make a choice. You can follow your friend's wishes and suffer the potential fallout from the bride's mom, or you can offer the bride a mellower, mom-friendly gathering. This is truly your own decision to make, and you should base it on your best judgment.

Mom Is In; Keep It Clean

Suppose the bride wants her mom and/or older female relatives to be invited. She realizes that certain things may be inappropriate, and you are essentially left to plan a tasteful bachelorette party. This is a cakewalk for you. All you need to do is avoid the strippers, sex toys, loud music, uncontrolled drinking, and inappropriate clothing.

Now, that's not to say that Aunt Betty doesn't know how to have a good time. Maybe she likes the corner tavern and her Manhattans on the rocks. You don't need to rule out everything. Just be aware that some families find blow-up dolls funny and some families don't. You and the bride should touch base about her family and any definite no-no's. Some older women really get a kick out of stuffing dollar bills into a phony cop's g-string. To each her own.

 ESSENTIAL

> One of your biggest concerns you will have as hostess is keeping your guests happy. You may be young and uninhibited, but you must also be respectful of the guests' feelings. Knowingly inviting a group of very conservative women to a party that is going to make them extremely uncomfortable isn't funny. It's inconsiderate.

However, if the bride's family is more conservative, perhaps you'll want to steer this party more in the direction of a luncheon or dinner. It won't really be a bachelorette party, but it's going to serve the same purpose—the bride will be the guest of honor, and will get a chance to relax and spend time with her female friends and relatives. If she hasn't had a shower, you may even want use that title and include the requisite rite of gift-giving. (See Chapter 5 for more on planning a joint shower/bachelorette party.)

What Do You Mean You Can't Come?

When you plan your guest list, keep in mind that not everyone you invite will be able to attend. Some guests will have to make the choice between attending the pre-wedding party or the wedding itself. Financial difficulties, a busy schedule, and work-related matters are just some of the real-life factors that may keep the women you invite from attending the bachelorette party. As the hostess, it's your job to remember that no matter how sick you are of hearing them, legitimate excuses are just that—legitimate. Accept that not every invited guest will be able to attend, no matter how hard the bride is crying over it.

However, in some cases an invited guest may need a little prompting from you. If a friend of the bride's lives a mile from the party and is blowing off the bachelorette party because it will be a dry event, maybe it's time to remind her that she's not going to a party to get wasted, but to wish the bride well. A little guilt goes a long way with some friends. With a few tactful words, you may just save the day—and the bride's friendship.

Chapter 7
That's Entertainment, Baby!

Bachelorette parties are often scenes of unbridled enthusiasm, but of course that all depends on the type of entertainment you're planning. If you're into the mellower scene, your entertainment options will differ greatly from wilder bachelorette parties. But "mellow" doesn't have to mean dull. Whatever your pleasure, there's fun out there just waiting for you to find it. Here are all the details!

It's Hot Stuff

Many bachelorette parties include some kind of risqué entertainment. It's often what women expect, and if your engaged pal is looking to unleash some pent-up pre-wedding anxiety and/or excitement, you're in luck. There are countless ways to liven up the bachelorette party, and plenty of willing commercial participants to help you in your quest.

How about Strippers?

The mere mention of the word *bachelorette* often elicits the following inquiries/admonitions:

"Are you going to a strip club?"
"Oh, you *have* to have a stripper!"
"What time are the male dancers arriving? I don't want to be late for that."

 FACT

If you live in the boondocks, a quick perusal of your phone book is unlikely to yield many clues as to your hunk-for-hire's where-abouts—unless you know where to look. A popular heading is "Entertainers," with sub-headings advertising a specialty in bachelor and bachelorette parties.

Male dancers have become something of a staple for many bachelorette party–planning books—the one thing that no one wants to exclude, and the one event of the evening that the guests will be sure to show up or stay for. As the hostess, it's your job to hunt down the stripper and provide him for the hungry audience. Think of it as bringing two worlds together in complete harmony. What he has, they want, and they are willing to pay for it—which is what he's after. It's a perfect union.

 ESSENTIAL

> Treat this as you would any other business transaction—get the name of your contact, and get everything possible in writing. If your stripper never shows, or he breezes in and out in five minutes flat, you'll want the terms of your agreement in black and white—or you may be paying for just a peek at those pecs.

If you're a hostess on the shy side, this may seem like a daunting task. Fortunately for you, it isn't. It takes a few phone calls—you will not have to visit the seedy side of Metropolis to find Officer Naughty, the (hopefully fake) cop who keeps losing his pants. He works for an agency, and he's waiting on pins and needles for your call. This is his job, and he has a car payment due.

Once you contact the agency, you should inquire about the following:

- **Cost.** Is everything included in a flat rate, or will a few extra bucks get you more? Your next question is what is their definition of *more*. More time, more skin, more *what*?
- **Forms of payment accepted.** You will most likely not be able to pay the stripper on the evening of the party with a credit card for the obvious reason that he won't have any pockets.
- **Length of stay.** Find out about how long the "entertainer" will stay at your party. Will there be an extra charge if he is unexpectedly delayed? If, for example, your guests want an encore, you don't want to get hit with a surprise charge. And you may not want the stripper to be hanging around after he's worn out his welcome. A reasonable time limit is a good thing.
- **Previewing the merchandise.** Is the entertainer performing anywhere where you could sneak a peek at his, um, work? If he's going to show up at a party in a bar, for example, you could be amongst the patrons there. If not, is there video of his performance? This may or may not be important to you, but some women want to make sure they're not going to get a less-than-perfect male specimen for their party. Take a moment and imagine the potential consequences of making *that* mistake.

- **Pick a theme.** You may be able to request that the stripper arrive dressed in specific garb. If the bride-to-be has a thing for rock stars, or meter readers, or cowboys, you can't go wrong with making a request for that specific costume.

Of course, a completely different and perhaps preferable route to finding a suitable male for display is to ask around. If you have a friend who's recently had a bachelorette party—or attended one—all you'll have to do is find out if the hunk in question was to everyone's liking. Not only are you getting a reference on an actual stripper, but you'll also be able to find out if the agency in question was professional and easy to deal with.

Out on the Town

If you're taking the ladies to a male dance club, call ahead and ask if they have a special rate for bachelorette parties. Some clubs are willing to work out special admission prices for you and your gal pals, especially if the party is a sizable one. Advise your girlfriends to bring along a fresh stack of dollar bills, which will come in handy for stuffing the undergarments of any male dancers within reach.

Don't Forget Your Manners

Although it may be near impossible to remember, the stripper is a human being. He could be your brother or your friend. He happens to be a whole lot hotter than any male friend you've ever had, but that's another issue. The object of the evening is not to humiliate the stripper. Have your fun with him and let him go.

Lest you think male strippers are not real people, consider Martin, who used to drop his trousers as a side job. "By the nature of the job, you've got to have a sense of humor," he says. "If you don't, you're going to take things way too seriously. But it's one thing to laugh with ladies who are acting all sex-starved—it's another when they're insulting you, calling you names like 'Meathead' and asking why you don't have a real job and all that. Like, why would you hire a guy just to insult him?"

 ALERT!

> If you are hiring a male dancer to perform at a party in a restaurant or other public place, check with the management *before* you make arrangements with the entertainment agency. Some locations will nix any proposal of scantily clothed men; others may put a time constraint on your plans.

The situations Martin describes are, by his own estimation, few and far between. Just make sure that your group is not crossing any lines between nuttiness and offensive behavior. Though you're looking at him as an object, he isn't one. He's really a person with friends and family and other interests besides taking off his clothes. Keep an eye on things and rein in anyone who's going a little too far with her comments.

Let the Games Begin

So you've planned the evening out. You have the stripper arriving at ten, you have your appetizers and drinks in the preparatory phases, you've got your music laid out . . . and still, you feel there's something missing. There's some downtime that you have nothing planned for. This is a major no-no called "dead air"—one of the worst things that can happen to a faltering party. On the off chance your party starts to waver and you need some filler, have some games planned.

Bride and Groom Trivia

Trivia games are always fun. Although you'll have to do some research to set up the questions, the payoff will be worth it. There are several variations of this game.

The first is simply Bride Trivia. Who knows the bride the best? The obvious answer may seem to be her family or her childhood friends, but that's not always the case. To set up this game, ask the bride some really obscure questions, like what type of shoes would she wear everywhere if it were socially acceptable? (You may be surprised to learn that your fashion maven friend would go barefoot—or wear her ratty slippers to work if she could.) What kind of work would she be doing if she had the chance to go back and change her college major?

The second variation of this game is a take on the Newlywed Game. You'll have to get the groom involved here. Ask him some questions: Does the bride prefer silver or gold (or platinum) jewelry? Where did they meet for the first time? What was their first conversation about? She'll undoubtedly give one answer, and you'll read the groom's very different responses. This is an opportunity for everyone to be in on the betrothed couple's relationship, and it may be a real eye-opener for those who thought they knew the pair well.

 ESSENTIAL

Trivia games are supposed to be fun for the guests, too. Don't veer off into subjects like the guy the bride would have married if only she hadn't been dumped by him a few years back. This type of thing may be offensive to the groom's family, especially if they're not close to the bride.

There are endless variations on the trivia genre. Where you want to go with it depends on the amount of time you want to put into planning it and the size of your party. If, for example, you and five girls are off to your cabin for the weekend, the questions and answers can be much different—more intriguing, more intimate, more detailed—than if you're playing this game in a group of fifty.

In a more intimate setting, you can even extend the questions to everyone. As Question Master, you'll separately (privately) ask everyone the same questions, then gather everyone back together. Read off the questions, and then read the stack of answers without revealing who said what. Let everyone guess who gave which answer.

Drunken Fun

Since any wild bachelorette party is going to include bottles and bottles of alcohol, you may want to put them to use and make the drinks a staple of your games. This is a win-win situation: You're filling time, and your guests will be so trashed after playing, they won't notice if you're providing any entertainment at all. There are so many drinking games, you probably couldn't play them all in your lifetime even if all you ever do is drink—just take a look online. You'll get a list you won't believe.

I Never . . .

The rules for this game are pretty simple. Each contestant has to admit something they've never done. For example, "I never went out to a bar without wearing underwear." Anyone who *has* ever left the house to do a little cruising au naturel has to drink. You are perfectly free to say you've never done something that you actually have—as long as you drink anyway. Hilarity will be the order of the evening as everyone watches who is taking a drink.

The key to this game is creativity. Think of the most bizarre things you've never—or ever—done. You may learn more about each other than you ever wanted to know, which is the whole point of this game.

 FACT

Drinking games are designed to break the ice (or to revive a dead party). If you're inviting vastly different personalities and you're a little concerned at how well they're all going to mix, introduce one or two of these games. The laughter that results ensures that strangers will be acting like the best of friends—at least for one night.

Celebrity Games

This is a great game with a lot of variations to it. Pick any genre. Actors, TV personalities, or people you actually know. Then, pick a category, like "people ever slept with" or, in the case of actors, "participation in movies that bombed."

Here's another example. You name a musician; the next player has to name a song. Others continue to name songs until you've exhausted the musician's catalog of recordings. Or name an oft-recorded song and try to name everyone who has recorded it. Name all the musicians who have died of drug- or alcohol-related causes. Pick a letter of the alphabet and name as many musicians as you can whose name starts with that letter. Whoever gets stumped, of course, drinks.

The Hour of Power

A note of warning: This game is geared toward guests who can hold their liquor. Guests drink a shot of beer every minute or two for an hour (adjust the time accordingly for your particular group).

An alternative is to substitute hard liquor *every fifteen minutes*.

Alphabet Games

There are two popular versions of stumping people with letters. The first is to pick a genre broad enough so that there actually are enough items in the genre to begin with every letter of the alphabet—geography is popular. Have everyone take turns naming an item in the genre, going in alphabetic order—Albany, Buffalo, Cleveland, and so on. At the end of the alphabet, start over. Whoever stops the alphabet train has to take a drink.

Another version of this game is to choose a genre and then each person has to come up with an answer that starts with the last letter of the previous answer. So, starting again with Albany, the next answer would have to start with Y—Ypsilanti, for example. And then the next answer would start with I. This game is a little trickier, especially after a few drinks.

ALERT!

The only way to ensure success with many of these games is to impose a time limit on answers. Give everyone five to ten seconds. If they can't answer, it's time for another drink.

Horror Shows

If you're married, pull out your wedding video. If not, ask a married friend to bring hers along. Every time the camera shows the bride's fake, nervous smile, everyone drinks. Or drink every time the hyperventilating groom wipes his brow. Or every time a drunken bridesmaid stumbles across the dance floor. Or every time one of the wedding guests calls the bride or the groom by the wrong name while wishing them well.

A great alternative is to pull out an old prom video, if you have one. Set your own rules and keep the wine flowing. It could be a painful show.

Very Adult Party Games

Many bachelorette parties have adult themes, with X-rated foods, male strippers, and even racy games. There is an abundance of paraphernalia available—enough to host a party every night for a week without repeating your games or decorations.

Scavenger Hunts

If an adult party is right up your alley, try dividing your guests into groups and having them hunt for fun party (adult) toys. You can be very creative in where you hide things, and watch your guests' consternation as they search and search. Just make sure you keep a list for yourself so that a future houseguest doesn't end up finding a plastic phallus in his or her pillowcase. If you're really generous, you can let your guests keep what they find.

If you have a whole weekend at your disposal, you can also make a list and send your guests out into the real world. Of course, you'll want to make sure that most of the items on their lists need to be purchased in adult stores—adding to your amusement and their embarrassment.

Get Your Blindfold

Another amusing little game is Pin the Organ on the Male. (Or maybe you can come up with a more creative title for this game.) Though there are actual party kits for this game, you can construct one yourself. All you need is a suggestive poster of a hunky—preferably barely clad, and somewhat cheesy—male, scissors, and construction paper. Imagination is your key ingredient here. Endow him with gifts any man would feel blessed to have.

Guess My Size

This is a variation on guessing how many jellybeans are in a candy jar, except that your guests will be guessing the exact measurement of the likeness of a manly buddy. Make sure you have a ruler with small enough increments so that you can get the exact size—it makes the game more interesting. The closest guess wins.

Hang a Piñata

What's more surprising than an extremely large (papier-mâché) male member hanging from your ceiling? The fact that it's filled with candies in the shape of a penis. Don't be surprised if you hear your guests yelling, "Oh my!"

Give out Prizes

The prizes for these games can be as entertaining as the games themselves. As your party is already steeped in sordidness, don't bother handing out tasteful prizes. If you're just not willing to part with the larger props you're using for your games, you can easily substitute smaller ones. Here are some ideas:

- Key chains with pictures of nude men.
- Liquid-filled pens that disrobe the little man inside when turned upside down.
- Any number of inexpensive phallic-shaped prizes: straws, ice-cube trays, goody bags filled with little manly candies.

QUESTION?

Where am I supposed to buy this stuff?
All the supplies you'll need for your games, as well as prizes and decorations, are available online and at adult stores. Some are even available in trendier gift shops.

Make Her Blush!

Since the bride is looking for some fun, you may as well go all out. Don't let her escape with her dignity 100 percent intact. She'll thank you later. Some ideas for maximum degradation follow.

Give the Bride a Hickey

Carry some flaming red lipstick with you. As the night progresses and your bachelorette group starts running into more and more drunken men, you can play Give the Bride a Hickey. Drunken men will usually not think twice about you applying lipstick to their mouths if it means they get to leave a mark on the bride's bod. Maximum embarrassment for him and her.

Sweet Success

Bring along some candy necklaces for all the girls. Only men can bite the candies off. (One candy per man.) First one with an empty string around her neck wins. Alternatively, the bride may sell her candies to men. They'll still have to bite them off, but they'll have to pay her a dollar or buy her a drink—whatever she wants.

Dress to Impress

In addition to the fake veil you're going to make the bride wear all evening, consider that perhaps she has a streetwalker side to her that she very rarely gets to show in public. Buy her some trashy items so that she may flaunt this side. Maybe she really *likes* pleather microminis and fishnet stockings. And who cares if she doesn't?

If she just won't go along with that, at least buy her a fun little T-shirt. There are countless to choose from, complete with fun little sayings printed on them, like "Bad Girl" or "Evil." If you just can't find the right garment in a store, make her a T-shirt that proclaims her status as a woman of questionable character. Think of an interesting catch phrase to scrawl on it—something like "Bride with No Pride." The more homemade this shirt looks, the better. And you should look for something extremely snug.

A Partner for the Night

The ultimate humiliation is handcuffing a blow-up doll to the bride and forcing her to carry "him" around all night. If you're really feeling creative, you could glue a picture of the groom's face in place of the doll's—not necessary, but a nice touch. Give him some undies (maybe a man thong) if you want—in fact, this may be funnier than letting him hang out all night.

ALERT!

Now stand back and look at what you've done to your friend. She's dressed like a hooker, with fake hickeys all over her, a damp and stretched out string around her neck, toting around a full-sized, naked blow-up doll. Plus she's hopelessly drunk. Are you happy? You should be. You've achieved near perfection.

Gifts for the Bride

What do you give the bride-to-be who has already been given everything? How about something indecent? The bachelorette party has sprouted a cottage industry of naughty gifts that you may not even know existed. There's a whole range of products out there: There are *kind of* naughty gifts that you could give even if your mother were present, and there are *extremely* naughty gifts that would make even the most adventurous blush. Choose wisely. If you're just not Internet savvy, these things can also be found in cheesy gift stores at the mall or in adult stores.

Body Works

The bride is embarking on a honeymoon soon (and, at least in her mind, she'll be on it for at least a year), so why not give her something to take along on her journey? Put together a kit of some nice body oils, massage tools, and an instructional book or video on sensual massage. Or get her a book on the Kamasutra and/or tantric sex. Musk is an interesting gift—one bottle for her, one for him. It's supposed to contain pheromones—scents that attract the opposite sex.

Yummy, Yummy

There are some foods that are considered aphrodisiacs—chocolates, caviar, and wine are some good examples. Put together a basket of these foods and present them to the bride as her bachelorette party gift. You can throw in a cookbook that deals specifically with these types of foods. Don't forget to include ginseng, which is easy to find these days, and is also supposed to have aphrodisiac effects. She'll love it, even if she doesn't know a colander from a stockpot.

Games as Gifts

There are plenty of "adult" games out there—from board games and dice games to all types of role-playing dress-up games—the objective being for the bride and groom to disrobe and get down to business. This genre extends into all types of adult accessories, like handcuffs, silk masks, edible undergarments, and oils—things that the newlyweds can use as props in games of their own creation. (The bride is not required to give you the details, by the way.)

Think of these gifts as marital aids. Things are bound to cool off between the bride and groom at some point. Games like these will add a little spice to their lives and keep things interesting. In fact, with gifts like these at their disposal, things may never cool off.

I See London, I See France

The gift-giving wouldn't be complete without some racy lingerie. There are so many areas and accoutrements to choose from—a bra with tassels, garter belt with fishnet stockings, crotchless panties, a thong with feather trim, or even a corset.

 ESSENTIAL

If you just can't bring yourself to purchase such a personal gift, get her a gift certificate to a lingerie shop. She can buy anything she wants then—nice or naughty. She can even take the groom along for kicks.

Take a friend and spend an hour or two in a lingerie shop. And don't bother trying to pick out something nice. She can do that on her own, but she probably won't buy anything trashy for herself. If you can't decide on anything else, get her some satin sheets. She'll definitely appreciate the gift. And you'll be sure to get a thank-you note from the groom.

If You Want to Keep It Clean

There are all sorts of pre-wedding gifts to give the bride. Of course, if she hasn't had a shower, you could give her anything she's registered for (or anything she needs, in the event that she's not registered at all). Since most brides are buried in cookware and crystal by the time their bachelorette parties roll around, look for something more whimsical—a hat, or a shirt, or cute little undies with "Bride" embroidered on it, for example.

 FACT

With her emotions already running high from the wedding preparations, these types of gifts are guaranteed to bring the bride—and possibly the guests—to tears. The bride will cherish these sentimental gifts long after she gets over the thrill of her wildly expensive china.

Have a picture of you and the bride, or the whole tight-knit group of her and her girlfriends, nicely matted and framed—a little memento of her single days, and a reminder that woman cannot live by man alone (not forever, anyway). If you're really into sentimental gifts, get all of the bride's closest friends to write her a little note about what she means to them. You can compile them into a scrapbook, along with pictures from the past.

Keeping It Fun

Of course, bachelorette parties are a blast. Many women rarely have a chance to cut loose and enjoy a night full of drunken craziness. However, you need to make sure that the evening turns out to be a safe one, too. And safety is one more thing that requires planning.

If you see a friend almost passing out from all the alcohol she's consumed, don't let her keep on drinking. This is common sense, of course, but it's also seriously dangerous. Hospitals have stomach pumps for a reason—you all need to watch out for one another so that none of you is hooked up to one by night's end.

Transportation is another safety issue during a night of drunken fun. Don't let your trashed friends walk home alone. You have many transportation options at your disposal, and these will be discussed more in Chapter 9.

 ALERT!

> Make sure that when the limo pulls away, you didn't leave anyone behind, and don't allow any of your girlfriends to leave with a sleazy guy you know she'd never look at twice if she were sober. Use the Buddy System. No one leaves the bar until everyone is present and accounted for.

The big thing to keep in mind is that you don't want anyone getting hurt. Look out for one another and have a plan to get everyone home safe and sound. That way, when everyone looks back on this bachelorette party, you'll remember how much fun you had. You won't have to remember some unfortunate event that ruined the party. Enough said.

Chapter 8

Theme Parties

Theme parties—you either love them or hate them. If you're not a big fan, it's worth remembering that these don't have to be tacky or overdone. It is in fact possible to have a tasteful, normal theme party—or you can go as far as your creative visions will take you. This chapter will cover theme suggestions, menu options, decorations, and invitations for your theme party.

A Word about Theme Parties

There are two types of hostesses: Those who love and depend on themed events, and those who absolutely cringe at the thought of them. Most people (hostesses and guests alike) tend to fall neatly into one category or the other. You either *have* to have matching table-cloths and napkins or you don't really see the point. No matter which side of the line you fall on, there is a theme and a structure out there for you to plan your party around.

Theme Lovers

You love parties. You love giving them, you love attending them, and you love everything about festive occasions. You're a Party-Planning Princess, and the envy of professional party planners everywhere, because you're a natural. You use your imagination freely and have countless ideas in your head.

 ALERT!

While themes have their purpose and are usually appreciated by guests, they can be a burden to someone who feels uncomfortable wearing a cowboy hat at your Western-themed party, or who doesn't particularly feel like speaking French all night long at your Parisian affair.

This is great, but you need to be aware that while themes are great party-planning tools, they have their dangerous side, too. Are people beginning to avoid your parties because they're a little overdone? Are you forcing people into situations where they're less than comfortable? There's a fine line between using a theme for planning purposes and *forcing* everyone to play roles of your choosing for the evening. That's going overboard.

Be aware of how far you're going with your idea. Are you using it to push guests to uncomfortable extremes? Avoid parties that are too rigid and structured—your guests will feel constrained and won't be able to let loose and enjoy the event, and some may run for the door, never to return. Make everyone feel welcome, including the folks who refuse to use the props you've placed by the entryway. In other words, don't pout if some guests refuse to do the twist and at your fifties party.

If a Theme Is Not Your Cup of Tea

Themes are just plain silly to you, and no one is going to convince you otherwise. Who wants to decorate the house in the likeness of a hacienda and serve Mexican food and drinks when you live in Minnesota and don't know *anyone* of Latino descent? It's just silly, you think. Silly, silly, silly. Themes are for dramatic people, you scoff.

Maybe your definition of "theme party" is too broad. Narrow it down a little. A theme just has to entail *one concept*. Themes centralize and organize your party. It may be easier to shop and plan for a gathering of any size if you have one Big Idea to work around. You don't have to take it to extremes. You don't have to have a mariachi band and sombreros for every guest.

The theme you pick would only extend to food, drinks, and possibly decorations, though you can hold off on that if you feel it's just too much. Activities that include theme games, theme music, and learning a foreign language are completely optional. If you do try a theme party, you'll be surprised at how smoothly your planning goes when you're looking at one idea instead of trying to gather concepts from all over the place.

 ESSENTIAL

If you find yourself as a guest at a party given by a Theme Lover, be kind. Don't sulk around telling all the other guests how stupid you think the party is. Your hostess went to a lot of trouble planning her party. No one forced you to come—and even if they did, that's still no excuse to be rude.

Choosing Your Core Concept

Whether you hate themes or just love them, it's best to look for a middle ground. Some of your guests will love themes, and some will hate them. You don't want to scare off either group, so *moderation* should the ultimate theme of your party plan.

Since your menu will be the most difficult (or at least the largest) thing to plan, it's a good place to start when choosing a theme. Get out your cookbooks, ask a friend, go online and find some recipes, or visit the local library. Find some ideas for food you can prepare or get from a catering service.

If you're going to be doing the food yourself, choose food themes that you can handle. Tex-Mex, for example, is an extremely easy way to go. It's fast and inexpensive, and it's *very* hard to make guacamole inedible. Since you're starting with the menu, you can easily change your theme to suit your culinary skills (or lack thereof) if you find that the food you've chosen is more advanced than you are.

 ALERT!

Don't forget that your menu is going to include drinks as well. Do a little research, get a little creative, and your party is going to be a hit. (For some ideas, check out Appendix B.)

Consider the Season

Next, think about when you're planning to host the party. Many themes are based on the weather, or on holidays that may take place around the time of the party. Is the bride getting married at the end of July?

Why not turn her bachelorette party into a Fourth of July barbecue? That's an easy theme to plan. Ribs on the grill, ice cream, flags, and sparklers. Done. Is the wedding set for November? Try a Halloween theme party.

If you decide on a bachelorette party tied to a seasonal theme, here are a few tips:

- **Find the right cookbook.** Many cookbooks deal specifically with the season or holiday you're working with. There are Christmas cookbooks, Halloween cookbooks, summer grilling-season cookbooks, and many more. It will be much easier to plan a menu using a book that's actually in step with your theme than it will be to pick through a huge book full of all kinds of recipes.

- **Shop early.** Don't wait until the week before your Valentine's Day party to shop for decorations. All the best merchandise will be sold out, and you'll be left cutting out construction-paper hearts for the next seven days solid.

- **Find some music.** Your party will be topped off when you have sounds of the season as background. For a party in the fall, try some bluegrass. For winter parties, try the traditional Christmas CD or some classical music. Summertime is the season of rock and roll. (You may have different tastes, but find a sound and keep the CD player going.)

Beach Party!

If you live near the water, and it's the middle of summer, what's better than a beach party? To make it even more interesting, you can go for a 1950s theme, when beach-blanket parties and movies were all the rage. Get your bikini top out, pouf that hair up, and apply your frosted pink lipstick, because you're going to listen to Frankie and Annette singing about fun beach times all night long.

Your menu for a beach party doesn't need to be complicated. Hot dogs, hamburgers, macaroni salad— any traditional, easy summertime fare is all right. Mix up a pitcher of iced tea (add a little vodka, if you want) and bring out your best red-and-white-checkered table-cloth. Plastic utensils and paper plates are not only welcome, but desirable. And as for entertainment, you can have some beach games ready, like volleyball and Frisbee.

Luau, Baby!

Another beach-themed party that you can hold indoors or out is the Hawaiian luau, complete with poi, pineapple, and roasted pig—or slabs of ham if you can't get your hands on a whole swine or if your lease prevents you from digging a roasting pit. If the girls don't want to wear grass skirts, they can easily find Hawaiian-print shirts. You can purchase plastic leis at any party store.

Get your Don Ho CD out. Play limbo. Drink piña coladas all night long, or at least stick a little umbrella in everyone's beer. Hang up the patio lanterns or light the tiki torches. Break out that ukulele. Find an instructional video on how to do the hula. Aloha!

It's the Bachelorette!

It may be that you'd like to stick to more traditional bachelorette party themes of sex and debauchery. Wild entertainment is covered more completely in Chapter 7, but it's worth revisiting here.

Since the theme itself is so socially unacceptable in any other situation, you might as well exploit it for one night. You probably won't get many more chances to blow up a man-doll and seat him at the head of your table, nor will you send guests searching for sex toys in your home on a regular basis.

 ESSENTIAL

If you're planning a joint bridal shower/bachelorette party, use the shower as your theme. If you're planning on letting loose after the gifts and the cake, and after all the relatives hit the road, keep the rowdiness down to a minimal level until you girls are alone.

There are companies out there that sell sex toys based on in-home sales (the concept is similar to hosting Tupperware parties). If you or a friend is interested in becoming entrepreneurs of this sort, you can host a sales party and tie it in with the bachelorette party. Everyone gets to see the products up close, and most will probably gain a real education in what's available for purchase.

Most women are hesitant to attend a sales party that is strictly about selling sex toys—for the simple reason that they don't want to be looking at these things in the presence of their friends and neighbors. Using it as a backdrop to a bachelorette is a different story. You're killing two birds with one stone here. You're providing a service to anyone who's interested, but more importantly, this is part of your entertainment for the evening. A word of warning: Be sure the bride is comfortable with this type of bachelorette party, and make it absolutely clear to the guests that they are not obligated to buy anything.

Looking for some decorations? Make them. Get yourself an issue or two of a male nudie magazine, and cut those pictures out. Mount them on cardboard. Place them wherever the mood strikes you. You might want to make a lovely centerpiece out of a few of them.

What's Cookin', Good Lookin'?

A bachelorette party theme doesn't have to make the more innocent guests blush. Remember, the purpose of the party is to prepare the bride for the upcoming wedding and married life. Since the bride is taking on domestic life soon, you may want to include a cooking lesson as part of her bachelorette party. This can be as formal as hiring an instructor (check the local schools for cooking teachers—they may teach on the side or know of someone who does) or as informal as you taking charge of the lesson.

 FACT

> The cooking-lesson theme works better with a smaller group for the obvious reason that fifty women will have a hard time crowding around the instructor in your kitchen. Your guests will lose interest very quickly if they're only *hearing* about what you're mixing up.

Decide what you're going to make and have enough space prepared so that all of your guests will have a hand in the creation. While you may not want to spend the evening cooking eight pies, you can hand off each part of the preparation to a different guest. The bonus to this is that you're preparing part of your menu as well, but make sure you have a backup plan in case your apple pie is burned to a crisp.

If the bride is a novice in the kitchen, keep the lesson simple. You don't want to overwhelm her and make her think she'll have to serve her new hubby cereal for every meal. And if you're hosting a coed party, the cooking lesson may be just as useful to the male guests.

Taste-Testing

A related idea is to have a party centered on one food, like chocolate. You can include the most decadent chocolate candies, as well as chocolate-covered fruits, nuts, and pretzels. Throw in a rich, heavy, seven-layer chocolate cake and you'll have a hard time getting anyone to leave—at least not until every scrap of food is gone.

You can have a party with pastries and cookies from around the globe, cheese and wine, fruit, pastas— you name it. Pick a food group and get creative with it. You'll surprise yourself with the number of ways you can serve even the most basic foods. Take pizza, for example. It is a perfect choice because it's easy and not a dish that anyone will be hesitant about trying. Try a chicken-topped pizza, a vegetable-topped pizza, a goat-cheese topped pizza—your options are endless. It's your theme. Take it anywhere you want.

Playing Dress-Up

Many theme parties have more to do with costumes and decorations than they do with food. Again, the sky is the limit here. The following are some basic ideas that can get you started as you brainstorm the perfect theme for your bachelorette party.

Period Parties

A period party takes a certain time period or era as its theme. These parties can be a lot of fun, particularly if you're choosing a time frame that's near and dear to your heart. When did you graduate from high school? Was it in the seventies or eighties or early nineties? Take a look in the back of your closet and howl in fright as you pull out those pants you used to wear—and you thought they made you look so cool. How about a party that celebrates those times long gone?

 ESSENTIAL

> Music for era parties is a cinch. Go to your local library if you're a little light on the music you're looking for. If you have an old record player and your LPs handy, so much the better. There's nothing like authenticity in the form of pops and scratches in your music.

You don't need to stick to an era you're familiar with. Choosing a fifties or sixties theme opens the door to all kinds of possibilities. You can get some peddle-pushers and a push-up bra to re-create your grandmother's girlhood look, or you can get some low-slung jeans and a peace medallion to capture the essence of your mom as a teenager. Or go where no woman has gone—into the future. What's your vision of fashion in the year 2100?

Menus for era-themed parties are pretty easy to put together. Every decade has its food. The fifties were all about casseroles, shish kebabs, and martinis. In the seventies, smorgasbords were huge. The eighties? Quiche, of course. Do your research and put together a blast from the past. You may find yourself wishing for a time transporter back to the days of innocence, punk rock, and pink hair.

Decorations for period-themed parties are no problem. If you're celebrating the times of your own adolescence, all you need to do is pull out some old pictures, preferably those that will embarrass at least some of your guests. You can decorate with any kitschy idea—movie posters, or odd artifacts from the time. A disco ball is perfect for a seventies party. How about a groovy lava lamp for your sixties-themed party?

Ethnic Parties

Is the bride a die-hard Scot? Is the groom's family from Greece? Ethnic-themed parties are a great way to celebrate the bride's and groom's individuality as a couple. Mixing a dual ethnic theme for a coed bachelor/bachelorette may shed a little light on their future as well. (She'll get a peek at what holidays will be like when she invites both families to her home—what *will* she serve?)

You don't have to pick a nationality belonging to the bride or groom. You can have a little fun here, and choose any country. Explore the culinary delights of Russia. Caviar and vodka? Your guests will surely be impressed. And who doesn't love French pastries and Brie? How about a Mexican fiesta? You won't find easier menus to purchase or prepare than these.

ESSENTIAL

> You'll want to include themed drinks in your menu. They don't need to be anything elaborate. French wine is easy to find. For a Mexican menu, try mixing up a pitcher of sangria. You'll also want to have lots of tequila and Mexican beer on hand. Just try to refrain from yelling *"Oui, oui!"* or *"Olay!"* every five minutes.

If you're thinking about decorations for an ethnic-themed party, be creative. One very easy idea is to re-create the colors of the country's flag in your table linens. It's tasteful, it's not going overboard, and it's a tribute to the nationality without crossing over into tackiness.

Your Friends Are Such Characters

How about a party where everyone comes dressed as a TV or movie character? You pick the time frame—it can be as broad as choosing *any* character, or as narrow as characters from the past year or two or from a certain genre. Adding to your theme, your menu will consist of movie or TV food—easy things like popcorn, candy, soda, junk food—and throw in some burritos and chips and dip for good measure. Have an "awards" ceremony at the end of the night for the best-dressed guest.

Another variation on this for a coed party is to pick a movie genre with clear-cut men's and women's roles.

Spy movies are good for this. The men come dressed as suave, mysterious types, and the women get to be their favorite sex kitten characters. (Lay down some rules: No packing heat and no bugging the room.) Whether the women want to use a suggestive pseudonym is up to them, but you can offer a prize for the most creative name.

Or you may want to go with a superhero theme. There are plenty of male and female characters to choose from, and you can find costumes at any costume shop. Codpieces and bullet-shaped bras will dominate the evening. Again, if you want to challenge your guests, offer a prize for the most creative brand-new superhero name, including a brief description of what he or she does in the name of justice.

Fill the room with fun decorations, like comic books and posters. Your menu can be pretty casual, as superheroes are always on the run—plan a wide variety of finger foods and appetizers.

Guess Who?

There's nothing like a good masquerade party. Each guest must keep her identity concealed until midnight. Trying to guess who's who is exciting and a little scary at the same time. This is especially fun at coed parties, when you think the man behind the mask is one person, and he turns out to be another—and although he was wearing that mask the whole time, it's clear he has eyes for you.

ALERT!

Don't try organizing a masquerade party with people who are averse to theme parties and/or mask wearing, as they'll blow their cover way before they should and take the fun out of the evening.

Masquerades tend to work best with larger groups, where the guests don't know each other's mannerisms and body shapes so well that they're easy clues. They're also most successful when they're combined with a costume theme—everyday clothes can be a dead giveaway, even when you don't know the person in question very well. Try to have your guests enter through an area where they can remain anonymous. Don't tell them to park in the driveway and come right in, where everyone can see the mysterious man who has emerged from Chad's bright yellow car.

Your menu for the evening can vary, but should be based on the type of costumes your guests are wearing. Have you asked them all to wear gowns and tuxedos? Your food will be a little more formal. Shrimp and crudités, Brie and caviar are some options, along with champagne. Or are they wearing costumes from the Halloween store? If so, your menu is much less formal, with breads and dips, fried appetizers and chips.

Since the guests are already decorated, you don't need to go overboard. If your guests are arriving in formal wear, you may want to break out that candelabra hidden away in your attic.

Las Vegas Night

If you and the girls just love to play games, make an evening of it. You can group into teams and challenge each other at board games, card games, dice games, scavenger hunts, bingo—whatever floats your boat. Have prizes ready for the winning teams and lots of finger foods handy for the quick energy boost your guests will need in between rounds.

 ESSENTIAL

Don't be surprised to see some of your guests waging competitive battles. Some women take their game-playing *very* seriously. Try to nip any serious hostility in the bud by moving on to a new game or suggesting an intermission.

Make another area of your home inviting and comfortable so that guests won't feel they have to stay next to the game boards the entire evening. Also set up your food in a separate area, away from the game playing, where worn-out contestants can take a break and mingle without breaking the other guests' concentration.

Paging Sherlock Holmes

Are your friends theatrical? Do they all get a little giddy over a good thriller? Host a Murder Mystery party, where one guest is "killed" and the others have to muddle through clues to find out who the culprit is. There are party kits available for purchase online or through game catalogs that will walk you through hosting a night of mayhem and murder.

The gist of this party is that your guests will arrive in character, which they'll be informed of in their invitations, and clues will be given via audio tape or CD throughout the evening. The whole thing is broken up into separate acts, which allows you to pace the evening according to your own timetable. At the end of the night, everyone will piece together their information and try to guess who the killer is.

Party packages come with everything you'll need—invitations, the audiotape or CD, a list of characters, a suggested menu (based on the setting of the mystery—is it 1800s London? 1960s California?), and notebooks for your guests to organize their clues in.

A Formal Affair

If your gathering consists of a small group of women who love the theater, the opera, the ballet, or the symphony, make that the center of your evening. Make yourselves glamorous and take the town by storm. Have a nice dinner before you take in the show. You may want to hire a limo for this evening, which will provide a nice "together" feel for before and after the event.

FACT

> The flip side of a night at the opera is a Western Hoe Down—perfect for the bride who's really into country music. You can hire an instructor to teach the latest Western line dances, decorate your house with a Southwestern desert theme (coyotes and cacti), and serve up some ribs and beans. And don't forget your cowboy boots and your ten-gallon hat.

A Few Coed Ideas

While the bride and groom are about to walk down the aisle, they may *not* be planning a Shotgun Wedding. Maybe you should plan one for their coed bachelor/bachelorette party. Think of it as a sort of rehearsal for the real thing. Won't they appreciate their real wedding so much more after this?

Suggest some outfits for your guests—men can come in their overalls if they want. Though women are far more reluctant to dress the part here, make sure the bride at least has a tattered veil to call her own for the evening. One caution: Tread *very* carefully here. Though many people find the Shotgun-Wedding theme amusing, it may be offensive to others.

You can go to the other extreme and plan a Royal-Wedding party. You don't need to go to the expense of renting formal gowns and tuxedos. Just treat the bride and groom like a prince and princess for the evening—don't forget her tiara and his crown. Cater to their every whim, and overdo it for the full effect.

If you really want to go all out, rent a red carpet runner from a florist for their entrance. Your can serve finger sandwiches and crumpets, along with spiked tea and champagne. Long live the queen, indeed!

Gotta Dance

Is the bride having nightmares about what the dance floor at her wedding is going to look like? Is she afraid that the groomsmen will stand around twiddling their thumbs so that no one knows they can't dance? Maybe you all want to learn the latest line dances. Host part of the coed party at a ballroom dance studio.

 FACT

> When it comes to dance lessons, you have a choice of several themes. Maybe you'd like to learn ballroom dancing, then host a dinner in a formal restaurant. Or maybe you'd like to learn the Salsa, and then head out to a Latin dance club.

Call ahead and reserve a block of time for your party. The bride and groom will pick up a few steps, and the bridesmaids will rest easy knowing their toes will be spared from the groomsmen's feet during the reception.

Hit the local tavern after dance class for a few brews and snacks. You've all earned it. Once you've refueled, you can all hit the dance floor and show the regulars what you've learned.

It's Still Sort of Greek to You

Are you getting the gang from college back together for the party? Make it a toga party, for old times' sake. Nothing in their pre-wedding schedule is going to be more fun for the bride and groom than wrapping themselves in sheets and wearing wreaths of grape leaves on their heads. In fact, go ahead and attach a veil to the bride's headdress.

You can go with the traditional keg for this party, but since you're all a little older, you may want to opt for actual bottles of beer, or mixed drinks, or wine. Tradition is a nice thing, but try mixing it with your new, more mature tastes.

If you're into the whole theme, you can try making Greek foods like fava dip, souvlaki, or pastitio. If you're really just trying to recapture your college days, all you need to do is prepare some junk food and dip.

Make It a Surprise

Your theme can be less about the decorations and more about the whole idea of the party. A surprise party, for example, doesn't really need an extra theme (though you can include one if you want)—it's all about the surprise. If you're planning a bridal shower/bachelorette combination party, you don't need to have a cowgirl theme, for example.

If you're planning on surprising the bride with a bachelorette party, there are a few guidelines for surprise parties you should follow:

- **Keep it on the Q.T.** Don't broadcast the event to everyone you meet. Make it very clear to all of your guests—via bold print on the invitations—that the bride is in the dark about the upcoming party.
- **Keep your head on straight.** With all the white lies you'll have to tell the bride just to keep this party a secret, you might lose track. Make some notes for yourself as to what you've told her. It sounds like a crazy thing to do, but if you're going to lie to anyone, you'd better have a great memory—or be very organized about it.
- **Snag the bride.** Make sure the reason you give her is compelling enough that she's actually going to show up at her own party. Asking her to come to your house because you need help painting may result in a flurry of last-minute excuses from the bride as to why she can't help out. Dangle a carrot in front of her—tell her you want her opinion on the wedding gift you bought for her. She'll show up.

ESSENTIAL

Surprise parties are not for everyone. If the bride is a bit shy or just doesn't like parties, think twice before hitting her with a great big chorus of "Surprise!" She may be more overwhelmed than excited by the whole thing, which may leave you feeling resentful after all the planning and plotting you've done for her.

Invitations

You've chosen a clever little theme for the bachelorette party—make your invitations just as clever. Make them attention-grabbers, and not just throwaway scraps of paper. You can purchase fun invites at a stationery store, or with the use of your computer you can create just about any kind of invitation that you can imagine.

As you think about the invitations, keep in mind that the most important thing is that you match the theme with the invitation. Don't send out beautiful, floral invitations for a beach party, or invitations with animals or seashells on them for a royal-wedding party. When your guests receive their invitations, they are going to get a feel not only for the party itself, but also for your level of organization. If a comprehensive theme is important to you, remember to carry it over with your invitations.

Let Your Creativity Loose

If you're the artistic type, you can use your skills to create your own unique invitations. And even if you're not artistic, there are computer programs available that will *make* you an artist.

Use your computer to make unique invitations. You can purchase special software for designing invitations, or just use regular paper decorated with wacky pictures or photographs you print off the Internet. If you've got a digital camera, you can also include a silly picture of the bride on the invites.

 ALERT!

> If you're trying this for the first time, give yourself plenty of leeway—you can always purchase invitations if the ones you're making don't turn out right. But you'll need enough time to determine if you need to make that purchase.

If you're not into computers, rubber stamps are a great alternative for making invitations. All you need are stamps, ink, and paper—you can create any kind of invitation that says anything you want it to say. There's almost no limit to what you can do. If you need help, go to a craft store and ask for some pointers (what kind of paper works best with what you have in mind, what type of adhesive you'll need, and so on). Have faith in your abilities and give it a shot.

Go Back to the Basics

If you just can't find the right invitations at the party store, you hate the whole stamping idea, and you're not comfortable sending out invitations via e-mail, get back to basics. Make those invitations from art supplies. All you really need is a good idea. The rest is a cakewalk, as long as you can master scissors and glue, and maybe a little glitter here and there.

For example, if you're thinking about having a fifties party, make some invitations that resemble poodle skirts, or better yet, a faceless bouffant. For a beach party, cut out some seashell invitations. Make a disco ball invitation for a seventies party. Create a glittery shoe invitation for an evening at a dance instructor's studio. A veil invitation is perfect for a wedding-theme party. For a wine-tasting party, all you need to do is create an invitation resembling a wineglass. Print the party information out neatly, and *voilà*–you're done. Another Creative Hostess Award goes up on your mantle.

Chapter 9
Getting There

You and the girls have one thing on your mind: fun, fun, fun. You have it all planned out—you're going out, or you're staying in, or you're taking off for the weekend or the night. You know *where* you're off to, but have you considered *how* you're going to get around? This chapter reviews your options for transportation and also offers some ideas for eliminating the need for transportation.

Get Professional Service

Many bachelorette parties turn into projects in painting the town red. Depending on where you live, there may be a few places you can count on—or a slew of hot spots worth visiting. Whatever the case, if you're planning on drinking, be smart. Don't drive.

 ESSENTIAL

> One of the most popular options for bachelorette parties is to hire a limo for the night. There are a variety of options available, including a superduper stretch limo, which can seat—believe it or not—fourteen wild women, or smaller versions that may seat only six.

Limo Perks

If you're planning a night of serious boogying and drinking, limos are the best way to ensure that everyone gets around safely. The added bonus to hiring a vehicle and driver is that you can think of the car as a little pit stop. Picture this: You're visiting the fifth club of the evening. It's two in the morning. The other girls are still going strong, but you're starting to feel a wave of fatigue washing over you. You need a little break from the action.

Luckily, you have a huge, private car waiting outside for you—and a driver who is watching it. You can safely retire to your vehicle and catch a few winks—just enough to revive your party spirits and allow you to rejoin the group, instead of going home and missing out on the rest of the party.

Some women have so much fun *in* the limo, they end up skimping on the bar scene. Marcy recalls her bachelorette party: "We hired this awesome stretch limo with everything in it—TV, DVD, CD player—you name it. We went to two bars, and I don't know if it was a slow night in town or if we just wanted to get our money's worth out of the limo, but we didn't stay in either place very long. We ended up just driving around for most of the night—laughing, singing, drinking, calling our boyfriends on the car phone. The driver dropped everyone off at my friend Sherry's house at midnight, but we weren't ready to go home yet, we were having so much fun!"

Plan Ahead

If you think hiring the limo would be perfect for your bachelorette party, you need to get down to business and start getting organized. First, you need to take the wedding season into consideration and plan accordingly. It may be the dead of winter as you're sitting and thinking about planning the bachelorette party, but you must fast-forward to spring or summer or next winter, when the wedding will be right around the corner. You will not be able to call a limo company on May 1 and book a limo for your friend's bachelorette party on May 15 (not unless some bride somewhere gets cold feet or a prom gets canceled). Limos are booked *way* in advance.

FACT

Generally speaking, you'll want to make your first call to the limo company as soon as possible. If you have lots of time at your disposal, don't feel funny about calling a year in advance—they'll let you know if they are booking that far in advance, and when to call back if they aren't.

Avoid Being Taken for a Ride

The limo of your dreams may or may not come equipped with a bar, TV, VCR, CD player, and a phone. If you're thinking about hiring a car, you may have visions of a night of luxury ahead of you. You can see it all now—you're lounging on leather seats, calling all of your friends (the ones who couldn't join the party— you wouldn't want them to miss out completely), sipping a martini while watching your favorite game show, all the while cruising around town. Now that's class!

But if you absolutely need to be surrounded by all the latest limo technology, do your homework thoroughly. Just because a company is listed under "limousine" in the phone book doesn't necessarily mean it fits *your* definition of luxury. Some limousine companies out there have an aging fleet of vehicles that would hardly meet your superior standards. Oh, there's a bench seat in there, but it's not leather; it's crushed velvet—and there's a curious stain in the middle of it. There's a phone, but it doesn't work. There's no TV. The whole interior has kind of a strange smell. Your driver is stopping to talk to strange people who seem to know him and the car well. This isn't your fantasy—it's your streetwalker nightmare.

Take a lesson from Kelly, who hired a limo for her friend's bachelorette party. "I looked in the phone book. All the ads looked the same, so I made a few calls and went with the cheapest company. This 'limo' was a bucket of rust. It was old, it was dirty, and the driver even seemed embarrassed about it. We had to provide our own liquor, so once we got loaded we could laugh about the car. If I had it to do again, though, I would shop around more and put the money toward a nicer limo service."

 ALERT!

Kelly's night was saved by the group's sense of humor. If your engaged friend has a limited ability to laugh in the face of adversity—and you know she won't see the irony in riding around in a "luxury" pimp-mobile—use your planning skills in the name of prevention.

Get Your Pen Ready

There are a slew of questions you'll want to ask your contact at the limo company. (If your limo service has a Web site, much of this information may be available to you there.) Have your planning notebook ready, and designate a few pages to this research. Give yourself plenty of room to write all the information on different companies so that you can easily compare and contrast services and prices.

First, you're going to get the name of the person you're talking to, as well as determine who this person is. Is he or she the owner? A driver? A person passing through the office who just happened to answer the phone? You don't want information from someone who shouldn't be giving it.

 FACT

> If you absolutely require that the driver be dressed in full chauffeur regalia, you need to specify your wishes. For less formal occasions like a bachelorette party, the company may only require your driver to be dressed in something a little more casual, like dress pants and a vest.

If the person you're speaking with is hemming and hawing and generally doesn't seem to know the business very well, you are well within your boundaries as a potential customer to nicely request another contact: "Is there someone else available who knows more about what a bachelorette package includes?"

If no one else is available at that time, feel free to

leave your name and number so that the person who actually deals with that side of the business can return your call. If you're getting nowhere fast with your inquiry, move on. You probably don't want to deal with a business like this anyway.

Get the Quote and All the Details

Price is a slippery subject here, and you want to nail it down quickly. If you've been given a quote, what does that price include? Some limo companies will give you a package price that will include the limo for a set number of hours, and then any extra time is charged above and beyond the price you're being given. Some companies will charge by the hour, but require a minimum number of hours. Larger limos will cost you more.

Find out if the quote includes "extras." Some companies include complementary snacks and beverages (alcoholic and nonalcoholic). Many will go out of their way to include your own special touches—things like balloons, chocolates, or caviar. You will end up footing the bill for these, but they'll do the legwork for you.

It's Time for an Inspection

Ask if you can look at the fleet of vehicles before making your decision. Do your investigative work very carefully here, as appearances can be deceiving. A brand-new limo that looks beautiful from the outside may look like junk once you take a seat inside. Likewise, a limo that looks a little older may have been completely refurbished with new seats and all the electronic gadgets you're after. And definitely don't shy away from asking to see the interior of the car you're inquiring about; after all, it's where you'll be spending a big chunk of your evening, not to mention your money.

Many limo companies will require you to give them a deposit for the evening at the time you are making your reservation. Most of the time, this deposit will be nonrefundable, which means that even if the bride breaks off her engagement, you aren't getting that money back.

 ALERT!

Ask a lot of questions, get everything in writing, and read everything you sign very carefully—especially the fine print. Although it may seem like no one really reads service contracts, you should. Save yourself a headache and a self-beating later.

Stretching Way Out

If a limo isn't your speed, check out a minibus or a modified SUV. Both have more seating room (they can fit about twenty people) than the typical limo, so you should expect to pay a little more for these vehicles. Also expect to be amazed when you step inside and realize just how huge those SUVs really are. And no, you shouldn't try to modify your truck to look like this just so you can look cool driving to the grocery store.

This type of vehicle may be just what you're looking for, especially if you're planning a coed party. There's lots of room to stretch out and get to know one another without being seated on top of one another—unless that's what you want—all the while cruising the town in an almost ridiculously large automobile. Fun times are all over your party map in this vehicle!

Gratuities

Some price quotes will include a gratuity of between 15 and 20 percent of the total bill. Other companies will leave the tip up to you. A word of advice: When you're figuring out the budget and how much the limo is going to end up costing you, factor in a healthy tip for the driver.

 ESSENTIAL

> Tipping isn't an area you should skimp on, especially if the driver has given you good service, and especially if you're going all out and hiring the best limo with all the extras. You're going to look like a huge cheapskate. Don't be surprised if you find tire tracks in your lawn the next morning.

Good service includes a driver who shows up on time. He knows when to chat up the group and when to stay out of the conversation. He gets you where you want to be, he's there when you come out, and he makes sure everyone is accounted for. He helps his inebriated clients in and out of the vehicle and he's polite. These are minimum requirements.

Good service does not include taking abuse in the form of teasing and/or harassment from the drunken women in the limo. It doesn't include being sent off to the drugstore or convenience store to buy you a new lipstick while you party the night away inside a club. It doesn't involve dancing with you or any of your guests, and it definitely isn't acceptable to ask the limo driver to perform the duties of the male stripper you didn't hire.

 QUESTION?

What if I don't believe in tipping?
If you're against tipping as a social practice, you really shouldn't patronize businesses that depend on tips. This includes restaurants, bars, hotels, and limo services—so if you don't like tipping, it looks like you're going to be staying home a lot.

While these things are nice perks (and things that some drivers will do), this is not what you've contracted this driver for. He's not your personal slave for the evening. Remember: You are *not* the star of a prime-time soap opera. You're only playing the part for an evening. This driver is not your personal employee.

If your driver has met the base requirements, tip him well. He's spent the whole evening catering to a bunch of rowdy, drunken women. He deserves a little something extra for that. Yes, he is being paid by the limo company, but if you hire a driver, you should be well aware of the fact that the drivers depend on making tips as a part of their salary.

If the driver turns out to be a real lout with a sexist mouth, a horrible sense of direction, and a curious habit of being missing in action every time you're looking for him to take you somewhere new, you may certainly adjust the tip accordingly. And if the driver is just plain awful, call the company and complain on the first business day following your party. They were supposed to provide you with a service; if they haven't met their end of the bargain, they may be willing to refund part of your money. (Don't bet on it, though.)

A More Informal Arrangement

It's possible you don't like car services, or maybe you just have to admit to yourself that you can't afford to spend so much on the limo because you're spending a lot on those funky decorations. Or maybe you forgot to call about the limo and now everything's booked solid. Don't despair! Here's where you get creative and come up with Plan B.

Call someone who isn't going to be offended by not being included in the bachelorette party—a man. Your brother or cousin or a good male friend may be convinced to act as your party's chauffer for the evening. You and the girls provide the vehicle (or vehicles, depending on the head count), and the driver will provide the sober, responsible driving.

Make sure the guy you sign up for the gig is trustworthy. Don't hire someone who has been in ten accidents in the past year—and check to see that he knows the area you're going to be traveling in. And remember that you need to make the job worth his while. He's going to be sitting outside the clubs waiting for a passel of drunken women all night. Some men might enjoy this, but more likely, it's going to be a long night for him. Pack him a bag of snacks, CDs, and magazines to pass the time. And don't forget the caffeinated drinks.

 ESSENTIAL

If this friend/driver is such a sweetheart that he refuses to take money from you, go the extra mile for him—especially if you've made him dress up like a chauffeur and called him "Bentley" all night. Get him a gift certificate from his favorite shop or restaurant.

Should We Take the Bus?

Maybe you're thinking that all this planning for transportation is just too much trouble. You live in a big city, and there are plenty of options as far as public transportation goes. What's wrong with taking the bus from the restaurant to the club and hitching a cab from the club to the hotel?

If that's your thinking, here's a word from the wise: You'd better come up with a better plan than using public transportation on Bachelorette Night. Many bus and train lines run only until a certain hour. In addition, do you really want to be sitting and waiting, depending on a bus or train that may or may not show up on time? If the subway or train line shuts down for any length of time, for example, what are you going to do? Sit in the station and drink? And how many cabs will all your guests need just to get home safely?

You also don't want to be on a bus going home after a night of indulgence and have that sudden wave of nausea hit you. The driver is probably not going to stop the bus route for you, and you're going to incur the wrath of the other passengers if you stink up the bus with the contents of your stomach.

Safety First

It's better to have your group's transportation planned out in advance, without depending on a bus or subway to get you where you need to be. It's worth the money for the convenience alone, and also for the safety concerns of the evening. What will happen to you (or one of your guests) if you miss the bus you wanted to take home or, worse, if you fall asleep on the subway by yourself?

These are not questions you want to find answers

to. You want to be smart, plan ahead, and make sure everyone safely gets where they need to be.

Just Stay Put

But maybe you don't need transportation at all. Instead, you can rent out a block of hotel rooms and go from there. In addition to being the best place to crash if you're out on the town and unable to drag yourself all the way home, hotels are a great place to keep your bachelorette party completely contained in one building—and without having to do a lick of work. Inns offer many of the same conveniences, but with a personalized touch. A nightcap in the lounge or hot cocoa in the parlor? It's your choice.

Check In to the Hotel

If getting out and *staying* out is the plan for your bachelorette evening, give some thought to booking a block of hotel rooms. Why drag yourselves all over town when you can find everything you need under one big roof? The beauty of many luxury hotels and resorts these days is that you could literally live in them without ever having to venture outside (as long as the delivery trucks keep making their stops).

There are hotels out there that are microcosms, generally located in or near large cities or tourist sites. Most of them are meant to lure out-of-towners, but don't let that scare you away. You're entering a little enclosed city where everything is clean, the air is seventy degrees, and you can find anything you need by asking the man at the front desk. Wouldn't life be great if it were more like this?

 ALERT!

> Keep the party in the designated areas of the hotel. Other paying guests do not want to hear you rocking and rolling all night long while they're trying to snooze. The hotel management has no qualms about removing unruly room partiers from the property, so be considerate of others.

In a place like this, you can book a few rooms—or better yet, a suite—and let the night take care of itself. You and the girls can check in sometime in the afternoon, work out in the exercise room (all right, you're not really going to do that—but you *could* if you wanted to), take a dip in the pool, and have a nice dinner in the five-star restaurant in Corridor One. Or perhaps a more casual dinner in the three-star restaurant in Corridor Two is more your style. Or maybe you're all the room service type.

A Great Way to Party

Now, although you're tempted to crack open that minibar and get the party started, there's no need. This hotel has nightclubs in Corridors Three through Eight!

You and the girls can get down all night long, and you won't need to go searching for your limo outside in the parking lot when you're done. Although, come to think of it, you *will* have to remember which floor and room number to return to, which will be challenging enough in a building of this size.

When you're tired, you're off to bed, which is a few minutes away, up the smooth elevator, and down the lovely climate-controlled walkway. The great thing is that you can even take a little nap and return to the action if you want to.

 QUESTION?

Got the gambling bug?
Try a casino resort. They have all the amenities of a luxury hotel, with the added bonus of an almost countless number of games and slot machines. You can spend all the money you win in one of their upscale boutiques.

When it comes to staying at a hotel, everything is right there for you—convenient and easy. No cooking, no cleaning, no worrying about how you're going to get home, no hassles. Have a great time and go to bed. Now, that's a great night on the "town," even if it's a fabricated, indoor town.

But booking some rooms in a hotel doesn't necessarily mean that you're planning a wild night. If you and the girls are coming from every which way, it's easy to use a hotel as a centrally located meeting place. You'll have a nice bachelorette dinner, a little bit of the nightlife, and then off to bed. No need to party all night long; maybe you'd rather sit and chat or take in a touristy sight nearby.

 FACT

> If you're booking a party of twenty women, make that *very* clear to the person taking the reservations. You don't want to end up scattered all over the hotel, and you don't want any misunderstandings—in the form of too few rooms being available—when you check in. You may also get a discounted rate.

Linda's bachelorette party turned out this way. "We were just all so busy, it was hard to pick a good time for a bachelorette party," she says. "Two of my closest friends were flight attendants at the time, and they were flying in and out of town—they were never around on weekends. We finally worked out a weeknight when all of the girls could get together. We booked some rooms in a nice hotel, had a really nice dinner, a few drinks, and a great breakfast together the next morning.

"No one had the time to plan and give a party, so this was the next best thing. It was low-key, but because we were all staying together it felt like college all over again. It was really fun, and we all got to be together, which was the entire point of the whole thing. I'm glad we did it that way."

By booking a few rooms in a hotel, you can basically cut down on a lot of the work involved in hosting a party and keep the fun going as late as you want. Just make sure the hotel is adequately equipped with the services you're after. Needless to say, don't try entertaining yourselves at the little motel, whose only amenity is the donut shop across the street—unless the point of your evening is to bore yourself to death.

A Cozier Getaway

Is a huge hotel not really your style? Do you cringe at the thought of devoting your bachelorette party budget to a huge, anonymous evening in a mini-city? Is the evening you're after a tame one?

Maybe you'd be better off booking rooms in a bed and breakfast or a small inn. These places cater to customers who prefer a more homey setting and the innkeepers are there for you—not for you and 500 other guests, but for you and maybe six or seven others. They will probably even know your name, which is something of an anomaly in the business world today.

Smaller inns may be a little pricier—often their prices are comparable to better-hotel rates—but the difference may be well worth it to you if personal attention and a quiet evening is what your group is craving.

You can expect home-cooked meals, one-on-one

conversation with the owners of the place, inquiries as to whether you have everything you'll need for the night (before you can ask for an extra towel, it may well appear on your bed), an individual feel to each room, and a relaxed, home-away-from-home atmosphere. *Very* different from the megahotel down the block.

Depending on the size of the inn and the size of your group, you may have the entire place to yourselves, which really lends to that feeling of being back in college or those high school sleepovers when parents were away. You can lounge in the parlor of the inn and chat the night away. Just don't expect room service all night long. Innkeepers have to sleep, too.

 ALERT!

> The inn isn't the place to get outrageously wild. This is actually someone else's home, and while they do open it up for business, you still need to be considerate of the fact that it's not a circus tent.

Another reason you'll want to be on your best behavior is that many quaint inns are filled with expensive antiques. You break 'em, you buy 'em. Even if you wanted to get the bride a beautiful antique lamp for her wedding, she'd probably prefer one that wasn't smashed.

It's a good idea to talk with the owners before you book any rooms in a smaller inn, and tell them what you're after. Discuss the following issues:

- **Length of stay.** Will you be arriving in the afternoon or late at night? When are you planning to leave?
- **Meals.** Will you be expecting dinner at the inn or are you planning to head out? Will you wake up for the early breakfast or do you prefer a late brunch?
- **Details of the plan.** Who will be coming with you; whether they're a loud bunch or well-behaved ladies; and whether you expect your party to run well into the night.

 ESSENTIAL

Staying overnight at a hotel or inn offers you the convenience of staying put and not worrying about how you're going to get from your house to the bars or restaurants and back again. It's also a great way to pick a central meeting place in the event that all the girls are coming in from all over. It's a hassle-free way to keep your bachelorette under one roof and let someone else take care of everything.

If the innkeepers aren't prepared to handle what you've got in mind, it's best to look for another place to go. Many innkeepers are incredibly flexible, but each inn has its own "house rules." Find one that suits you.

A Weekend Trip

In Chapter 4, you were introduced to the idea of turning your bachelorette party into a weekend affair. If checking in and out of a hotel within twenty-four hours seems too rushed for you and your friends—and providing everyone's schedule can accommodate a two- or three-night party—you may be looking for something more.

When considering the transportation for your out-of-town adventure, ask yourself this: Do you want to maximize your time at your destination, or is getting there really part of the fun?

Obviously, if you just want to get to your intended location, you're going to want to pick the fastest mode of transportation. Make sure that it's also economically feasible for everyone. Don't assume that everyone will want to hop a plane to go to the mountains, when you could drive there in two hours for a lot less cash. Look into the possibility of cashing in some of those frequent-flyer miles if cost is an issue.

If, on the other hand, you intend to make the trip part of the whole bachelorette party experience, plan out your course. Are you going to rent a car? How large a vehicle will you need? If it's going to take days to drive to that casino or beach house, where are you going to stay along the way? Are there tourist attractions dotting your route? Don't go rushing past Graceland just because you don't personally have a thing for Elvis. There are some things you just *have* to see. And if the trip really is the best part of the adventure you're embarking on, why not just rent a big RV? Now *there's* an idea.

 ALERT!

> If you're having a hard time finding a good deal on your own, talk to a travel agent. Because they know every nook and cranny of the business, they can often work wonders with your budget, even after you've tried everything to cut costs.

Have the Party at Home

If you're having the party at home, you won't have to deal with trying to figure out how to get anywhere. You'll be staying in, playing randy games, nibbling on suggestive-looking snacks, playing wild bachelorette games, and drinking to your hearts' content. Who needs to go anywhere when you have a party like this planned? *This* is where the action is!

Since you won't be leaving the confines of your Party Palace, you don't need to worry about trans-portation issues for the entertainment portion of your evening. However, you *do* need to consider how your guests are going to get home safely. Luckily, you have a few options:

- You can prepare a list of cab companies and their phone numbers so that no inebriated guest needs to fumble through the phone book later.
- You can hire a friend to shuttle your guests home. (Again, this would be someone who is an obvious noninvite, such as a male friend.)
- You can let anyone who's had too much fun (or too much to drink) spend the night at your home. You may cringe at the thought of having to deal with hungover guests in the morning, but it's a better alternative than someone getting hurt.

Host a Sleepover

One benefit to an at-home sleepover is that it's perfect for the short-notice bachelorette party. You can throw this evening together on just several days' notice if you have to, as opposed to having to book rooms weeks or months in advance at a hotel or an inn.

 ESSENTIAL

If you're inviting guests to spend the night, you're not obligated to cook an enormous breakfast in the morning. You've provided entertainment and lodging for everyone. They won't mind eating cold cereal or toast. You're not *really* an innkeeper, after all.

And consider this: Guests can arrive when they want, they can stay the night if they want (but they're not obligated, as they would be if they were paying for a hotel room), and there's no one who's telling you to quiet down—unless you have pesky neighbors who can't stand any noise past 10 P.M.

Chapter 10
A Reality Check

Bachelorette Night fast approaches. You've done your planning and can see it all now: You're going to have appetizers and drinks at home, you're going out in a limo after that, you're going to hit all the hot spots, and you girls are all going to look so pretty, people will be blinded by your beauty. Someone needs to come back down to Earth—you.

Don't Expect a Perfect Party

You're excited. The bride's excited. And you both should be. It's her bachelorette party, you're all planning on having a crazy night filled with more fun times than you can shake a stick at. While it's natural to look forward to good times, having an *exact* idea of how the evening is going to turn out is a dangerous thing to do. High expectations can lead to more fun, but they can also lead to bitter disappointment if things don't turn out exactly right.

 FACT

Unfortunately, large last-minute problems can crop up for no apparent reason. Even the best-prepared hostess can't control everything. On the brighter side, there's nothing out there you can't handle. Just keep your cool and deal with whatever comes your way.

Where's My Food?

It's the afternoon of the bachelorette party. You're hanging decorations, you're dusting, and you're making everything *just so*. Things are coming along smoothly, and then it happens. The phone rings. The caterer has the flu and won't be delivering the crab cakes and oysters you've ordered.

Don't throw the phone at the wall or out the window. You'll break it, and the caterer still won't be showing up. Here's where you find out what you're made of. Don't freak out.

 ESSENTIAL

> In the event of a last-minute food-related emergency, your table may not be set exactly the way you had planned, but as long as you provide something decent for your guests to nosh on, it won't matter to anyone (except you) that your fancy caterer didn't show up.

Choose an easy menu you can put together at least partially by yourself—you can go for Mexican dips (salsa, guacamole, sour cream) and chips. You can throw together quesadillas at a moment's notice. Beef up the spread with some frozen foods—cheese sticks, chicken wings, whatever you can find that looks decent. Call the pizza place down the street and order a party pizza or sandwich platter.

This happened to Rachel right before the bachelorette party she was hosting, except her caterer skipped town and took her money with him. "I found out the day before that this business was defunct," she recalls. "I had twenty-four hours to come up with a plan for feeding fifty women. It really wasn't that hard, actually, with all the take-out places available. I just ordered some of this, some of that, more of this, and more of that. I picked up a cake in the bakery of a grocery store, and grabbed the nicest disposable plates and plastic eating utensils I could find. If I had known that it isn't that hard to do all of that, I might not have called the caterer in the first place."

Where Are My Wheels?

The man on the phone tells you that his entire fleet of limousines was destroyed by a garage fire last night. You're out of luck for the bachelorette party tonight.

You have some options here. You can rework your entire party and move it completely into your home—go with the easiest appetizers and the simplest decorations, get a caterer on the line, clean your house, and hang decorations all in one day. You're going to put way too much pressure on yourself, and without a lot of extra help, you won't get it all done. And you definitely won't have any energy left to enjoy the party.

The other option you have is to keep the party as planned. You can still go out on the town—you need to find a driver, though. If you can't find a male friend who's willing to break his plans for the evening to cart you girls around, consider cutting back on the number of clubs you're going to visit and call a cab instead.

Where's the Bride?

You've got the bachelorette party all planned for this weekend. Everything's been confirmed—you're doing the food yourself and you have plenty of supplies for replenishment in case you run low, and you're staying in and having a raunchy party complete with a stripper.

And then the phone rings. It's the bride, and she's home with the flu, or worse, she's decided she's not going to marry Mr. Perfect after all. The first thought that comes to your mind is, "What am I going to do with all this food?!" No, you're not a terrible person for thinking this way.

If the bride is sick, rescheduling is your best option, as long as she's sure she has another free night available before the wedding. (If she cancels twice, you have every right to stick her head into the dip.) Depending on the size of the guest list, it might be a very easy thing to do, or it might take you all day just to reach everyone.

 FACT

> Don't expect everything to go perfectly, even if you've been organized and on top of things from the get-go. You can't control other people, and as long as you're depending on others, there's always a potential for mishaps. And that's not even including things you have absolutely no control over—like the weather and home appliances.

In the event that the bride has called off the wedding altogether, you have two options, and the one you choose depends on the situation at hand. If she's upset about her broken engagement and feels the world has come to a screeching halt, cancel that party. Don't talk about it, don't ask her if she wants a pound of shrimp from your freezer, and don't mention how much money you spent on preparations. When she's over her grief, she'll realize how much you did for her, and if you haven't made her feel worse by rubbing it in her face (intentionally or not), she'll be all the more grateful.

If, on the other hand, she doesn't seem all that affected by her sudden change in life plans (to some women, it's only a relief to break off a bad engagement, no matter how close to the wedding they are), ask her if it's all right to go ahead with the party on the night planned. Obviously, it won't be a bachelorette party, but you can still have all of your guests over and have them eat all that food. Call the guests, of course, and tell them of the slight change in plans so that no one feels out of the loop or deceived when they show up at your door.

Marielle broke off her engagement three weeks before her wedding—and just a week before her bachelorette party, but the party went on as scheduled. She explains: "It wasn't that I was so heartbroken. My fiancé and I both kind of knew, I think, that we weren't going to make it in the long run, so it was better to call off the wedding than to get into a messy marriage and all of that. My bridesmaids planned my bachelorette party for months—and they went all out. They reserved a room in a restaurant, they hired a stripper, they invited almost sixty women—and all of that money was nonrefundable.

"I just couldn't see calling it all off and pretending that I was sitting home crying my eyes out when I really would have been sitting home feeling sick over the money they had lost for nothing. So we changed it to just a Girls' Night Out party. I wasn't the guest of honor—I was just a guest. It really was fine with me and a much better alternative to hiding out at my house that night."

More Trouble

There are a hundred things—big and small—that can go wrong. A blizzard blows into town, making roads impassable. Your dishwasher suddenly starts spitting out suds. The stripper who arrives at your house is a buxom bunny. Your male construction-worker dancer is at a bachelor party somewhere across town (and probably not having the night he planned on, either).

The important issue is how you react to any obstacles that suddenly pop up in your party's path. Keep your cool. This party is not the end-all, be-all of the world. Think of any problems as a little game—the object is to find the best solution in the least amount of time. If you can do that, you'll be miles ahead of other hostesses who sit and cry when the going gets tough.

Acceptable Behavior

Bachelorette parties are kind of strange. Often, the atmosphere encourages rowdy behavior and socially unacceptable practices, like playing games with sex toys. The twist here, of course, is that these things *are* acceptable within the confines of the party—to a point. So where do you draw the line? In such a wild atmosphere, how can you determine if things are getting out of control?

When It's Time to Take Control

Are you stopping the fun prematurely or are you saving your party from becoming tomorrow's headline in the local paper? "Local Bachelorette Spins Wildly Out of Control, Everyone Arrested"—you don't want that to be you. Unfortunately, you can't always rely on your own judgment, as you may either tend to fall on the very conservative side of things and object to guests using profanity, or on the wildly liberal side, like allowing your guests to go topless.

 ESSENTIAL

These are your best guideposts to determining where to draw the line on behavior at a party. You may *feel* like a party pooper when you turn the music down after midnight, but it has to be done if you don't want a cop on your doorstep—and this one is not going to take his shirt off.

The answer, then, has to lie in your surroundings. It's time to consider the following questions:

- How are the majority of your guests responding to what's going on? Are throngs of women headed for the door because one of your friends is getting it on with the stripper in plain view? That's one clear sign that the party is getting out of control.
- Is anything happening that could become a legal issue for you? If your guests are cranking up your stereo at three in the morning and harassing your neighbors who are knocking on the door to complain, you may have bigger problems in days to come.
- Is anyone putting herself in danger? If you are out in a bar and one of your friends is practically passing out while talking to some weirdo, it's time to move on—or take that limo home.

Even the Stripper Is Uncomfortable

First, you need to assess your own value system and compare it with the party you've planned and the guests you've invited. If you're a reserved person who is planning a sex-themed bachelorette party complete with a stripper and a big, inflatable penis as the centerpiece on your hors d'oeuvres table, you're entering unfamiliar territory.

Your guests are already being pushed in the direction of getting crazy. Don't judge them if they're making raunchy jokes and being a little more suggestive with your decorations than you're comfortable with. You certainly can't expect serious comments on how light and fluffy your cake turned out.

 ALERT!

> Keep in mind that your guests are going to have their own perceptions of your party intentions—anyone who decorates her home with male members and bakes a cake in the shape of Mr. Winky is setting a mood, willingly or not. It's not fair for you to get annoyed with the inevitable snickering of your guests.

However, if your guests are using your props to put on some sort of show (riding your inflatable centerpiece, for example) or are driven by lust and alcohol to attack the stripper, they are crossing the line. Have a word privately with any objectionably behaving guest. Though you may be dying to embarrass her in front of everyone, she's still your guest, so avoid a confrontation right in the middle of the party.

If you've spoken to your wild guest nicely and she's still out of control, you may be at a loss for what to do next. Don't lose your cool. First, try removing the impetus of the misbehavior—remind the stripper that it's time for him to leave, take some of the decorations out of the room, and make sure this guest doesn't get any more of that spiked punch. Then, try to move her into a mellower group's conversation, which may have a sedating effect and bring her under control.

The real problems occur when you have a group of guests who are feeding off of one another's behavior, trying to one-up each other. This one is doing her own striptease in front of the hired stripper, that one is seeing how many fake penises she can stuff in her pants, that other one over there is purposely trying to embarrass your quieter guests by telling them shocking sex stories.

When your party takes on a mob mentality of clearly over-the-line behavior, you're going to need help. Ask the bride to step in and talk to them; you invited them at her request, after all. This will usually do the trick. Even though you're the hostess and it's your house, the bride is running the show this evening.

Boy, She's Really Thirsty

Alcohol is another issue. You may not drink at all, or only drink in moderation. Other women love to imbibe and are not going to stop at one or two drinks—or five, or eight—and before you know it, they've lost count.

The bachelorette party is the time to let loose—not to lose control. Making a moral judgment is unfair, especially in this type of setting, but if any of your guests are so drunk that they can't stand up, they should be cut off, and you should definitely make sure they're not in possession of their car keys.

Again, you may need the bride to step in and have a word if this guest is becoming really offensive to your well-behaved guests—who will be actively shunning her, which is not adding to the ideal party atmosphere, either. Do everything possible to avoid a confrontation with a nasty, drunken guest, but if all else fails, call her a cab and send her on her way. One (extremely) rotten apple shouldn't spoil the evening for everyone else.

 FACT

> When a guest is obviously loaded and exhibits your average, run-of-the-mill obnoxious behavior—getting nasty or being way too loud or offending other guests—she's probably well past the point of being able to taste the alcohol in her drink. Be her personal attendant and get her the nonalcoholic version of whatever she's drinking.

If you're out on the town and one of the girls is getting loopy and out of hand, keep on eye on her. There are more dangers lurking in the shadows of the nightlife than there are in your living room. Don't let some creepy guy hang all over her, and don't let her leave with any strangers. These are stories that really do make the papers. Prevention is the key to avoiding those headlines.

Keep Your Chin Up

So things are going horribly wrong. You have drunken guests and sober guests at each others' throats, your neighbors are complaining about the noise, the bride is crying because you forgot to display her engagement picture, and you dropped the cake on the floor. "Great party," you're thinking as you shove through your guests to get into your kitchen, where you can hopefully smash a plate or two and feel better. "When will these people get out of my house?"

Hold it right there. Sorry to tell you this, but as the hostess, you are obligated to smile your way through this evening. That's one of the duties you agreed to when you offered to throw this party. You've invited all of these people to your home, and they took time out of their lives to show up. There's *nothing* worse to a guest than a sour-faced hostess who doesn't bother to hide the fact that she wishes everyone would leave—not the smashed cake all over the floor, not the bratty bride, not the crabby neighbors, and not even the sloppy, drunken guests.

 ALERT!

You will have plenty of time to have it out with the bride, your neighbors, and your drunken guests later—the middle of the party is not the time to address your major issues with anyone. Your stress level is much too high to think rationally about a fair solution. Do what you can to solve the immediate issue, and deal with any larger ones tomorrow.

So if you've offered to host a party, keep that smile going and be nice—no matter what goes wrong or who gets on your bad side. This will all be over soon enough. You're earning your hostess stripes.

Keeping Your Party Stress-Free

The best way to prevent problems is preparation. This includes informing your neighbors that you're having a party and asking them to let you know if the music is too loud, instead of calling the cops. It includes keeping an eye on the atmosphere at your party and knowing which guest is on the verge of turning into a drunken idiot. It includes talking to the bride and asking her if there are any details she forgot to mention and if there are any other things she just has to have for her bachelorette party, so that she won't have to stomp her feet and throw a hissy fit during her party.

It's also helpful to work on a timetable to keep yourself organized. Here are some milestones for planning your friend's bachelorette party:

- **Six months to a year in advance:** Start calling around and booking limos, restaurants, caterers, hotel rooms—any service you'll be paying for. It's especially important to have this amount of leeway if the bachelorette party is going to fall during the busy wedding months (spring and summer).
- **Three months in advance:** Start thinking about your

menu and your theme, if you choose to have one. Now's a good time to start looking for that stripper, too.

- **Two months in advance:** If you're planning on ordering any decorations or gifts from the Internet, don't put it off much longer. You need to allow for shipping and for the possibility of exchanges.

- **One month in advance:** You should have a blueprint by now—the place, the theme, the decorations, the entertainment. If you haven't nailed down your final menu and/or you haven't hit the party store to buy your decorations, get moving now. Your invitations should be leaving your hands now—in one bundle. Don't send half of your invites this week and half next week. People talk. Anyone who gets a tardy invite is going to feel slighted.

- **Two weeks in advance:** Start calling and confirming your arrangements with the limo service, the caterer, the hotel or inn, and the stripper. Get confirmation numbers, if possible, and the name of the person you're speaking to. This is likely to be your last contact with them before the big night, and you want all your ducks in a row.

- **The week of the party:** Get going early enough so that you won't be rushing the night before. If you're making food that can be frozen, great—you can start cooking now. Get your house cleaned, your decorations ready to go, door prizes wrapped, and games planned. Don't leave all these preparations to be done the day of the party.

FACT

Confirming at least two weeks ahead before the party gives you time to work out any problems. Let's say you call the limo service and they tell you you're booked for the pink limo—but you wanted the black one. You march right down to that limo company with your contract in hand and point out where the color of the limo was specified. With two weeks still ahead of them, the company should make arrangements for you to get what you booked.

Parties that have been well planned tend to take care of themselves. Yes, there can still be the occasional unforeseen glitch, but if you've taken care of business, one glitch will seem very manageable. It's when you've forgotten to make arrangements and try to do everything at once that things can go haywire.

Farming Out Responsibilities

Just because you've agreed to provide the place and food for the party, does that mean that you have to wear a maid's uniform and play the part? The outfit may be going overboard, but you should expect to do the lion's share of the work. That's why you're the hostess—you're in charge.

However, some women can't bear the thought of having to serve all night long and instead come up with alternative plans. Maria was a first-time hostess who was worried sick over having twenty women in her home. She decided to make things informal for everyone. "When people walked in my door, I showed them where the food was and where the drinks were," she says. "I told everyone that my house was their house, and they were entitled to anything in the fridge or the kitchen, and that if they couldn't find me and they needed something, they should go ahead and grab it. It worked out great. Everyone felt really comfortable, and I felt like no one was waiting around for a lime wedge or pretzels."

While Maria's notion is an interesting one, you should be careful not to take it to extremes. Telling your guests to get things themselves can be seen as, well, making them get everything themselves. In Maria's defense, she was not sitting around all night—she was hard at work, so having someone jump in and refill the pretzel bowl when it needed to be refilled was very helpful to her. This type of "open-door" hostess policy will work best in small, close-knit groups of women who already feel comfortable going through your cabinets.

Get Me out of This Kitchen!

Another way to make sure you're not tied to the stove all night long is to plan only part of the evening at your house. By starting the evening off at home—nibbling a little, having a few drinks, opening some gifts—

and moving it to a nightclub later, the bride is getting the best of both worlds, and so will you. She'll enjoy a more personal affair at your house first and you'll get rave reviews for your dip—along with knowing that your party time at home is limited. Later, you'll all enjoy turning the town on its ear. And you can leave your apron at home.

Don't Forget about Yourself

You're doing so much for your friend. You're working very hard to give her a great sendoff. You've made all the calls, you've dealt with all the headaches, you've interviewed strippers (poor you!), you're working with the groomsmen for an amicable coed party. . . .

It's so easy to get lost in the tornado of planning a party. In fact, if you don't slow down enough to take everything in on the night of the bachelorette party, you may wake up the following morning and wonder what the heck happened.

Take a page from Erin's book. She was the Superhostess. She planned, she cooked, she cleaned, she called guests who didn't RSVP, she served food and drinks, and she kept the whole party going. It was a great success.

However, she has a few regrets. "I feel like I missed the entire bachelorette party," she says. "I was so anal about everything being done at exactly the right time on the night of the party, and I had such strong ideas about stuff like where people should be mingling early in the evening, and where they should be mingling after dinner—how crazy is that?

 ALERT!

> If you feel that you're getting sidetracked by all the details and can't slow down, take a moment to remember why it was exactly that you decided to host the bachelorette party in the first place. Keeping those reasons in your mind may just be enough to keep your priorities straight!

"I wanted the food to look just right, so I kept rearranging everything. I wanted the ice to be well stocked, so I was icing the bar all night long—I was basically nuts. And you know what? I didn't have a good time. I didn't have a bad time. I just was in this little party-planning atmosphere all by myself. I wouldn't do that again—not after all the time it takes to put together something like this."

Don't forget to take the time to enjoy yourself. You've done all the work, and now it's time to reap some of the benefits. Of course, you have certain responsibilities to take care of during the evening—like keeping up with that darn ice, replenishing food and drink, and keeping an eye on your guests—but don't let it take up every single second of your night. You're a part of the party, too. Don't miss out.

Calling It Off?

Sometimes, despite your best intentions, you find yourself losing ground with every hostess step you take. You can't get a caterer for the price you want, there isn't a limo available within a ninety-mile radius, and the bride is acting like a brat, anyway. You're ready to call it quits. Quite frankly, you don't have the time or the energy to expend on something that is just blowing up in your face.

 FACT

Whether or not you knew anything about arranging a bachelorette party before you agreed to do it, headaches can be part of the territory, so quitting because you just can't take it is a pretty weak plea. If you offer this excuse to the bride, you should erase her wedding date from your calendar, because your invitation will probably get lost in the mail.

Think twice—no, think *three* times (at least) before backing out of hosting a party. This is a big deal, and not something you should do unless you absolutely, positively have to. If, for example, several major family crises have popped up in your life since you agreed to take on the responsibility for organizing this party, that's a pretty good excuse. But if you're just generally annoyed with the whole process, consider—and reconsider—this move and its probable consequences carefully before you tell the bride that you won't continue on in your role as the bachelorette party hostess.

Don't Give Up!

Before you quit, really mull over whether your excuse is a valid one. If, as in the case of a family emergency, you have other obligations you absolutely have to attend to, at least try to find someone to take over the planning for you. If the bride has a big wedding party, it shouldn't be hard to track down another bridesmaid to do the honors.

No matter how you feel about party planning at this point, you have to remember that your friend is counting on you to host what will most likely be the only bachelorette party she will ever have—and she's counting on you because you said you'd do it. It would be really unfair of you to back out simply because it's more work than you planned on. Keep on keepin' on. You'll be glad you did when this bachelorette party goes down in local lore as one of the best your town has ever seen.

Chapter 11

Human Hazards

The best and most experienced hostesses will tell you that no matter how much planning and preparation you put into a party, there is one factor that you will never be able to completely control *or* prepare for—your guests. This chapter presents some real-life bachelorette party disasters, and how the real-life hostesses and brides handled them.

Bachelorette Disaster Stories

The following stories are presented not to scare you, but to show what *seemingly* rational, normal people are sometimes capable of. The lesson to be learned from these anecdotes is that you shouldn't expect too much—from *anyone*. Always be on alert, and be prepared to take action. Put on your Superhostess cape, and have some ibuprofen handy.

I Had Him First

Lorie was hosting her sister Terry's bachelorette party. Terry had had a dubious dating career in that she had never been very picky about men—she kind of dated whoever was interested in her. Because she was nearing the age that she felt was appropriate for marriage—in other words, she wanted to be married by the time she was thirty—she made a play for the ring with Alan, a man everyone knew.

Well, apparently, a lot of women knew Alan *very* well. Once the drinking games began at Terry's party, it was revealed that not one, not two, and not even three, but *four* of the guests present had had previous intimate relations with the groom. One of the women also revealed that Alan was the best man she'd ever, um, "known."

Terry was understandably upset, as she'd had no idea how popular Alan had been with her own friends before he met her. In fact, she was so incensed, she left her guests to have a little chat with her man.

Lorie, meanwhile, was left to pick up the pieces of the bachelorette party. She says: "I didn't know what to do. These were women who had known Terry for years and years—and I couldn't blame them for any of the Alan stuff. I mean, none of them knew that Terry would end up engaged to him. But I did blame them for blurting out all of this information at her bachelorette party. That was just so wrong.

 ESSENTIAL

Don't worry, most of your guests will be well-behaved, respectable people, but every now and then, there's a wild card or two in the bunch—someone who will, surprisingly or not, throw a wrench into the works. Because bachelorette parties naturally precede a wedding, emotions sometimes run rampant, which can mean trouble.

"Terry had been engaged for six months—if they *had* to tell her, they should have done it earlier. I can't say it came as a complete shock to anyone that Alan had gotten around, but it seemed like a rude thing for her friends to tell twenty other guests the details.

"I ended up telling the four of them exactly what I thought, and I quietly asked—well, *told*—them to leave. I didn't want to make a huge scene, but my blood was boiling. And at that point, everyone else left, too, because obviously the party was over. Terry was gone, I was furious, and too much had been said."

The moral here? There is none. There's nothing you can do if a guest decides to share her intimate knowledge of the groom at the bachelorette party. You obviously can't interrogate your guests at the door, and you can't put tape over their mouths. Just beware that in small towns—or among small groups of friends—pasts are sometimes more intertwined than you realize. If you suspect something is up, you may want to broach the matter before your guests get drunk and play truth or dare.

 QUESTION?

If the guests start making confessions the bride doesn't want to hear, what should I do?
First, stay calm. It's not worth it to flip out and attack the big-mouths. Calmly tell them that they are acting inappropriately and ask them to leave. If the culprits have driven the bride to tears, that's hardly an overreaction on your part—being kicked out is exactly what they deserve.

She Had Him First, Part Two

Oh, men and their pasts. Who can keep track? Here is another tale of bachelorette party woe you can hopefully learn from.

Maddy and her girlfriends were getting down at a trendy club on Bachelorette Night. Her wedding to Rick was only two weeks away, and she was positively glowing with excitement. Things were going really well—her friends had appropriately embarrassed her by dressing her in tacky, suggestive eveningwear, and men had been buying her shots all night.

But Maddy was in for a sobering experience. Rick's old girlfriend entered the scene and started harassing the bachelorette group, calling Maddy some really horrifying names and claiming to be the mother of Rick's child. She even passed around the child's picture, although it was later revealed to be photo of a friend's child. Worse than that, the ex said she was seeing Rick behind Maddy's back and that the wedding would never happen.

 FACT

The emotional foundation of weddings brings out the very, *very* worst in some people. Strange revelations find the light of day and secrets are suddenly unearthed—and not always for good reasons. When this happens during the bachelorette party you're hosting, it automatically becomes your concern.

Needless to say, the night came to a screeching halt. Though the former girlfriend was ushered out of the bar by the bouncer (the scene she made was *that* bad), Maddy was shaken. Although her girlfriends assured her that Rick would have told her if he had had a child, she wanted to see Rick and find out what the story was.

Maddy's story has a happy ending. The former girlfriend really *was* crazy and had not taken the breakup with Rick well. He did not have a child with her, and he had no plans to leave Maddy at the altar for any other woman.

Is there a lesson to be learned here? Yes, actually there is, and it goes beyond a symposium on mental health issues. The mistake many people make in dealing with others is that they give them the same benefit of the doubt that one would allow any rational person. The lesson here is that there are many, many people out there who just are not rational. Fortunately, a healthy dose of skepticism is all you need to spot a wacko—in this case, the former girlfriend. Any woman who charges in to a nightclub to lay a whopping dose of the "truth" on anyone, and especially on a stranger, has issues.

Maddy was understandably disturbed. And, unfortunately, the former girlfriend won this battle by disrupting the bachelorette party—but she didn't win the war. Maddy knew that Rick was telling her the truth, and the wedding went on as planned. The former girlfriend has no doubt moved on to make trouble for another ex-boyfriend of hers.

This Way Out

Your responsibilities in a situation like this vary. If the bride is a very close friend or relative of yours, your reaction is understandably going to be much stronger than if she's a coworker or your cousin's fiancée, in part because you'll be better acquainted with her relationship with the groom—you'll have a feeling as to whether the "stunning revelation" is true or if the person making it is a liar.

 ESSENTIAL

Whether or not you're dealing with a creative storyteller, the fact is that it's just plain inappropriate for guests to make accusations or tell sordid tales about the groom at the bride's bachelorette party. Perhaps these guests have never read a book about polite party behavior, but since you have, you can call them on it.

How you handle a guest like this depends on the situation at hand. Obviously, if you're in a nightclub, it's not really up to you if the offending guest stays or goes—that's in the hands of a higher power (he's about eight feet tall and he's standing by the door). And if you can't get the higher power to help, why not move the party to another location?

If the bachelorette party is held in your own home,

you have the right to protect the bride from distasteful and hurtful remarks about the man she intends to spend the rest of her life with. That is, you have every right to ask offending guests to leave your home. The most effective way to do this is to remain very calm, even though you're incredibly peeved. If you're screaming at the guest and she's screaming right back, nothing will be accomplished—except a whole lot of screaming.

Following this logic, it's best to take the culprit aside and tell her quietly that she's upset the bride and she needs to leave. Singling her out in a group of fiteen women is going to lead to comments from the peanut gallery and more headaches for you. Sure, she's going to grouse about being kicked out, but let her look like the troublemaker she is. You don't need to sully your image by sinking to her level.

Don't Overdo It

Before giving a guest the boot, you need to make sure that the offense is absolutely, unmistakably huge. You should not ask someone to leave your house because she hates the bride's china pattern. And don't demand that someone go home because she hates the food you've made. The bride can easily avoid these guests, and they're not doing any real, irreparable harm.

The litmus test for removing a guest under these circumstances *must* be that she is trying to come between the bride and the groom in some way. Being generally annoying is an unfortunate trait, right alongside talking too much and dressing badly—but these *are not* good reasons for tossing someone out the door. If, in addition to or in place of these characteristics, a guest drops a major bombshell on the bride, open that door and clear a landing space—there's a guest coming through at maximum velocity.

Dealing with the Green-Eyed Monster

If only life were less catty. . . . There will be scores of women who are actually happy for the bride and her impending matrimony, but there will always be at least one woman who is seething with envy. It never fails. She may be an ex-girlfriend of the groom's; she may be an unlucky-in-love sibling or friend of the bride; she may be a friend who resents the groom's intrusion into her world with the bride.

There are at least a hundred reasons for jealousy, which is why it's so rampant, especially around weddings. It's a fact of life, and usually envy simmers below the surface and fades with time. But when jealousy rears its ugly head at the bachelorette party you're hosting, it becomes your issue to deal with, at least temporarily.

You're Happy . . . And I Hate You

Someone's good fortune is always someone else's deep misery. Anna, for example, lucked out when she met Donald several years ago. He's a good-looking guy, smart, nice, and loaded. He was prepared to give her the type of life most of us only see in magazines. (A pair of $600 shoes? Anna wears them to the grocery store—on her maid's day off, that is.)

Naturally, she was very excited, especially since she had hardly been raised in luxury. Her dad had passed away when she was very young and her mom had struggled—to say the least—to provide for Anna and her siblings. Anna's friends, who had for years watched her family's struggles to overcome their misfortune, were delighted that she was going to be able to put her financial demons to rest.

Make That *Most* of Her Friends

Kimmy had been right there alongside Anna during the hard years, too, but she was anything but happy for her. In fact, she had very little to say about Donald and the wedding, even though she was a bridesmaid and planning the bachelorette party with several other girls. Unusual behavior for Kimmy, yes, but no one thought much of it.

Bachelorette night arrived, with all the guests swarming around the bride, playing some naughty games, eating the great appetizers the bridesmaids had worked so hard to prepare. When the time came to play Bride Trivia, someone asked Anna what it was that first attracted her to Donald. Anna said it was his sense of humor. Kimmy, completely drunk at this point, disputed that answer. "Money!" she screamed, half joking.

When the other guests politely ignored her outburst, Kimmy vaguely recalls that she wouldn't let it drop: "I said something to the effect that if Donald was a bricklayer, she would never have gotten to know whether he had a sense of humor or not, because she never would have spoken to him in the first place." On and on and on it went, until Kimmy was ushered out of the room and eventually taken home by one of the other bridesmaids.

 ESSENTIAL

> It is regrettable that Kimmy didn't express her feelings to anyone. Maybe if she had talked to another friend before the bachelorette party, she would have remained at the party she was cohosting.

Was it embarrassing? "Oh yeah," Kimmy says. "The worst part was that I couldn't pretend that it never happened. Thirty other people heard it, and Anna was just *so* mad at me. To say that being a bridesmaid in that wedding was the most uncomfortable thing I've ever done is not an understatement.

"The thing is, though, I'm so *not* jealous of her anymore. I was jealous of the money, and that was it. I wasn't in love with Donald or anything. Now that I'm out and making money on my own and loving my job, I realize I can be well off one day too—which makes me feel even worse about the whole thing."

So what should you do with a guest who suddenly explodes in a fit of hostility? What about a friend who has been treated badly by men and wants to warn the bride? How about someone who truly believes that the bride is making a huge mistake and the bachelorette party is the perfect time to tell her?

Can you prevent these women from opening their big yaps, especially if they've been relatively well-behaved up until now? Of course you can't. But you do have the final word on what sort of behavior is allowed to continue at the party.

 FACT

> Kimmy was shown the door because she was rude, loud, and belligerent. As a hostess, you have every right to spare your other guests and the bride from "a Kimmy." That's a pretty black-and-white situation.

I'm Not Upset . . . *Really*

While Kimmy's jealousy eventually manifested itself in an outburst of epic proportions, many jealous friends or relatives may never really admit how they feel—not to the bride and not to themselves. This guest won't accuse the bride of being a gold digger at her bachelorette party. She won't come out and say that the bride is so lucky and that all she wants is to find the happiness the bride has found.

This woman will seethe quietly and resent the bride for every *other* thing she does—from the colors she has chosen for her wedding (horrendous) to the date of her wedding (very inconvenient). She'll hate the way the bride has been acting since she's been engaged—which may be a valid complaint, but it also may *not* be. She'll say the bride has changed, and she'll resent the groom and any new face in the crowd, like the groom's sister or friend.

What can you do with a guest who's jealous behavior isn't as deafening? This is actually an *easier* situation than handling someone like Kimmy. You can take one look at this friend and predict how she's going to act at the bachelorette party—she's going to hate everything. She's going to be sullen and picky, and she's going to loudly voice her disparaging opinions. She may try to take the entire party over and gear the conversation toward herself. Her entire plan is to draw attention away from the bride and make herself the focal point of the evening. Yes, she's going to be one of those difficult guests.

 ESSENTIAL

Granted, a friend like this may actually be struggling with the fact that her life hasn't turned out the way she wanted—but she might also be a manipulative nitwit. She needs to realize that she is not the *intended* focal point of the evening—and you may have to be the one to assist her in that revelation.

Your defense is to remain in control. *You're* the hostess. *You* call the shots (along with the bride, of course). You're not going to spend the evening playing Jealous Friend Trivia. You're not going to spend the evening discussing the jealous friend's life and times. You're not going to have a two-hour conversation on how unfair it is that the jealous friend hasn't found the love of her life yet. And if she sheds any tears, you need to pull her aside and have a private chat.

Whatever the case, a friend's bachelorette party is *not* the appropriate place to air grievances concerning life. The other guests did not make the trek to this party to hear a dissertation of woe from another guest. And this topic of conversation can really put a damper on your game of Pin the Doo-dad on the Naked Man.

You control what happens here. You must find a way to stem the hemorrage of complaints from this guest. Some suggestions:

- Feel free to jump in and redirect the conversation toward a general topic or toward the bride.
- Keep any comments you make neutral so that you aren't adding fuel to her fire. If she tells you how awful the food is, you either say nothing or suggest something more to her liking. Telling her to shut her pie hole is only going to give her something else to rail against.
- Kill her with kindness. You won't change her attitude, but you may prevent a Kimmy-like scene.

Jealous Siblings

Here's a breed set apart from the everyday jealous guest—and potentially twice as nasty. The jealous sibling is so dangerous precisely because she's family. If she's the bride's sister, you can bet this wedding is only rubbing salt in old familial wounds. If she's the groom's jealous sister, there's nothing the bride will ever be able to do to prove she's worthy of marrying into the family.

 FACT

Jealous siblings are usually hardheaded and hardhearted guests. They have their own agendas, which is to let the bride *know* they're not happy about her good fortune. They differ greatly from the jealous friend who's in denial—these girls are well aware of what they're doing.

You're going to have to take a different approach altogether in dealing with jealous siblings. Pretending they don't exist is unfortunately not an option. The bride's sister will most likely have to be invited to a large bachelorette party. Her absence will be obvious no matter what size party you're throwing, and not inviting her will only give her ammunition to use against the bride at a later date.

So what are you supposed to do when she shows up acting all nasty and spiteful? Run interference. Don't even give her the chance to make her hurtful comments and ruin her sister's night. If you have to, keep her as far away from the bride as you can. This is your lot in life—at least for this evening. Accept it.

Because you and the sibling both know what she's up to, she'll catch on to you pretty quickly. She'll either get fed up and choose to leave (hooray for you) or she'll stick around and give you a *real* run for your money.

 ESSENTIAL

> What you don't want to do is leave this sister completely unattended for the night. Sisters who fight like cats and dogs can turn a pre-wedding party into a dirty-laundry festival. The stink will follow you and your guests for months.

The groom's sister is a slightly different story, in that her motivations are different. Patricia married Edwin three years ago. Edwin is the only son and the baby of his family, and was practically raised as royalty by his mother and sisters. Perhaps they never expected Edwin to leave home, or maybe they were looking for someone a little different for an in-law, but, as Patricia says, "They got me, and I'm not going anywhere. So they better learn to deal with me or hit the bricks."

At Patricia's combination bachelorette party/bridal shower, Edwin's sister took special care to announce the cost of each gift that Patricia received. She then commented on the fact that Patricia was planning a very large wedding, considering she was paying her student loans off at the time.

"It was just so rude," Patricia says. "And embarrassing. I *knew* what the gifts cost—I was the one who registered for them, obviously. Everyone else knew what they cost, because they had all *seen* the registry and bought the gifts. So calling out the prices like a cashier in a grocery store was an odd thing for her to do, to say the least. She was trying to make me look like a greedy bride. It made *her* look like a petty, jealous person.

"And her comment about the cost of my wedding was ridiculous. Edwin and I both paid for our own wedding. We pay our own bills, including my student loans. We have never asked for a penny from his parents, and we certainly have never asked his sister for help, so our finances are none of her business. The real issue, as far as she was concerned, was whether it was fair for Edwin to take on my student loans—and that's also none of her business."

Obviously, the bad blood that already existed betweeen Patricia and her future sister-in-law was exacerbated by the sister-in-law's rude comments. So, if you're the hostess in a situation similar to this one, what are you supposed to do? Actually, you have several options:

- Make a lighthearted joke out of the whole thing and say something like, "Wow, do you watch a lot of those TV shopping channels? I've never seen anyone nail prices like you can!" She might get the point and put a cork in it.
- Keep her engaged in conversation or ask her to help out at the bar, so that she doesn't have a chance to comment on *anything*.
- If you're feeling bold enough to get in the middle of this sniper-fest, you can quietly mention to her that nastiness toward the bride is really in bad taste.

 ALERT!

If you choose to reprimand the unhappy sister, don't expect her to thank you for your etiquette lesson. Unfortunately, this is one of those heartburn-inducing situations. The bride is already on thin ice with the family, and any reprimands from her friends will most likely worsen the situation.

Luckily, the good thing here is that nasty comments from the groom's family are usually seen for what they are—pure pettiness. Because the groom's family is likely to be significantly outnumbered by the bride's friends and family at the bacherlorette party, the cold-shoulder treatment is just as effective in protecting the bride from further verbal abuse.

You don't have to have a formal huddle to inform your well-behaved guests that no one should speak to the groom's sister anymore. Any friend of the bride will want to distance herself from someone who is so mean-spirited.

 QUESTION?

Isn't it petty to shut out the groom's sister?
Sure. But in a situation like this, you don't have much of a choice. Being nice will more likely give her an air of confidence—she's being nasty *and* people are still being nice to her. Why would she stop?

Unless you're personally willing to take on the baggage that goes along with confronting her, you're out of options. A confrontation will almost surely include an airing of true feelings between the bride and her future sister-in-law, which is not something that should ever be done a few weeks before the wedding—or at least not without a licensed therapist standing by. This is the last thing you want the bride to have to deal with at her bachelorette party. You can fight fire with fire, or you can smother it.

An Unwelcome Guest

It's great if you plan a coed bachelor/bachelorette party that includes the bride, groom, and all of their friends—these are great get-togethers for the group that wants to be together. However, what if the plan is to have separate parties, but either the bride or the groom doesn't believe in "separate"? If the bride and groom are not on the same page, it's a real drag when one shows up to crash the other's party.

Men Who Crash (and Burn)

Missy had a bad feeling on the night of her bachelorette party. She just knew that she wasn't going to have a night with the girls *alone*. Her fiancé Wes was acting awfully funny and a little too supportive of the whole thing, being that he was, in Missy's words, "a control freak."

The girls went out as planned, but who do you suppose showed up at the nightclub where they were drinking and allowing men to nibble on their candy necklaces? Missy was furious and embarrassed: "You know, your bachelorette party is supposed to be this night to cut loose and let whatever happen. I looked up from where I was sitting, and there was Wes, just sitting at the bar watching me. And all I was doing was having a good time, but of course, it led to this huge thing—was I fooling around with someone? Was I looking for a last fling? Why was I dressed the way I was? He ruined the whole night for me, and honestly, I *still* resent it."

While you obviously can't lock the groom in a closet on bachelorette night (no, really—you *can't*), there are some ways to avoid inadvertently sharing the evening with him. Prevention and common sense are the keys to eliminating this problem. If, for example, you know the groom has control issues, don't volunteer information about the bachelorette party to him or to his friends. This seems like an obvious thing, but sometimes hostesses get so excited about the rowdy night they're planning, they can't help themselves. To a guy like this, listening to you planning how out of control the bachelorette night is going to be is not the least bit amusing.

 FACT

Diplomacy and tactfulness—rather than full-blown hostility—are your friends here. Angering the groom by nastily telling him the bachelorette party plans are none of his business is going to lead to big-time headaches for a bride who is engaged to a controlling, insecure sort.

If he's asking a lot of questions, simply answer, "I don't know where we're going yet. It's all kind of up in the air." It's not his party, and he's not on the guest list, so you are not obligated to tell him a thing about it—but you don't want to make an enemy of your friend's almost-husband, either.

Remember, unless he's physically abusive, it's not up to you to offer your opinion on her mate. She'll be forced to choose between her loyalty to her man and her desire to have a good time.

If you sense a real problem on the horizon with a groom who has to know everything about where you're all going and what you'll be doing all night, plan a surprise bachelorette. He can't be a spy if he doesn't have a clue.

If Your Bride's the Spy

Now, having covered this territory, reverse the situations. Women should likewise respect the men's right to a night out. The bride should trust that the groom is going to behave himself at his bachelor party. Don't allow yourself to be enlisted in any schemes to follow the guys to a strip club. It makes every woman involved look incredibly immature. If the bride really doesn't trust her groom, that's something she needs to address with him one-on-one.

 ALERT!

The absolute worst thing to do is to get yourself caught up in the middle of a pre-wedding drama. The groom won't think it's funny when he sees his bride standing sentinel at the door of the bar he's in—he'll think she's controlling and insecure, and anyone who's with her won't fare much better.

It bears repeating: Your poor opinion of her mate is *not* something you should express. Tagging along to spy on a bachelor party only proves (to the groom, if to no one else) that you don't think very much of this man. Stay out of it.

Someone Stop That Bride!

You don't want the groom following you girls around on Bachelorette Night—that's a given. But it shouldn't be because you're afraid he'll catch the bride doing something that would change his mind about marrying her. You want to go out and have some fun, maybe teetering on the edge of naughtiness, but certainly not crossing any lines. Don't give the groom anything to grieve over. While you obviously can't control the bride's every move, you should be on the lookout for signs of trouble. Dressing her up like a streetwalker is supposed to be a humorous prank. If she starts acting the part, reel her in.

No matter what age the bride is, no matter how many relationships she's had, she shouldn't be cruising for a last fling on the night of her bachelorette party. If you see it happening, that's something you need to address. You're hosting a bachelorette party to send her off into a new life with her soon-to-be-husband—you're not advocating her sowing her last oats.

Because you're the hostess and whatever happens at the bachelorette is going to reflect on you—fair or not, that's reality—you have every right to put your two cents in here. This is a *major* issue, and the ramifications of it are far-reaching. If something should go wrong, you're going to be on the groom's hit list and anyone else who hears the story probably won't take your side. Again, it may not be fair or accurate, but it's what usually happens in situations like these. The hostess bears at least part of the blame.

 FACT

When it comes to curtailing the bride from getting too wild at her bachelorette party, be aware that if you get involved, the bride may thank you later, or she may be mad at you forever. But either way, you'll know you've done your part and tried to settle things down a bit, and that's really all you can do, short of pulling out the hose on her and her new friend.

Chapter 12
The Party's Over

The morning after the bachelorette party, you wake to remember that you had such a great time . . . or that nothing went as planned . . . or that you remember nothing at all. You're either reveling in the victory of hosting an unforgettable party, or you're swearing off parties altogether. And now the bride is acting all funny. Will you two remain friends now that she's looking off to the future and you don't seem to be a part of it?

What You've Accomplished

So your party was a smashing success, you say. Everyone had a blast, the food was awesome, the stripper was foxy, and you didn't pay too much for anything. Before you go into the party-planning business, you need to appraise your evening honestly. By doing this, you'll have a clear picture of what to do and what not to do the next time you're planning a party.

Good Planning, Good Luck

There's nothing wrong with luck, but you can't count on it every time you host a party. As you probably learned from your experience of hosting this bachelorette party, planning is really the best way to prepare yourself—making sure you're getting the best prices, knowing who has called to RSVP and who hasn't, having enough food and drink on hand, and so on.

 ALERT!

While you need to accept the possibility of bad luck, don't leave everything up to chance. If you're inviting people anywhere, you should prepare to show them a good time. But you also have to roll with the punches. Remember: You can't control everything, but you *can* control your reaction to life's little mishaps.

Nevertheless, there is something else you need for your party to be a success. And that something is simply good luck. Even if you hired a stripper months in advance and call several times to confirm the reservation, he may still cancel on you at the last minute. If you have good luck, though, the agency may send an even manlier man to entertain you and your squealing guests.

Franny hosted a bachelorette party that was completely fueled by luck. "I was so lax in planning," she says now. "I had no business having people to my house with so little preparation. But people showed up with a plates of food, people showed up with wine and beer, and a lot of the girls brought CDs. If they hadn't brought those things, we would have eaten chips and dip—and that's all—and we would have run out of beer by about nine o'clock. Plus we would have had to listen to the same two CDs I had in the stereo, over and over."

Franny must have had a guardian hostess looking out for her. Imagine how her party would have ended up without the other guests' contributions—things that were a nice thought, but not anything a hostess should depend on. Franny's reputation for being a procrastinator may have prompted her guests to carry the ball for her, but you shouldn't expect the same treatment. Though it's polite for a guest to bring the hostess a small gift—a bottle of wine or flowers—it's not expected of them to provide the food and entertainment, so don't count on this happening at your party.

What did Franny learn from this experience? "I learned that I will never leave a party to chance again. It actually scared me to realize how unprepared I was. The amount of food these women brought was incredible—and it was gone at the end of the night. If I ever have another party, I will definitely plan a little better for it."

Except for That One Thing . . .

If the party went well, except for the fact that the buffet table collapsed, killing all the hors d'oeuvres in the process, and then you lost your mind yelling and screaming at your cohostesses and swearing like a sailor, then it's fair to say things didn't go all *that* well. Learning to accept a party for what it is—a fairly frivolous event, and not something that mankind is dependent on for its survival—is also part of being a good hostess.

 ESSENTIAL

You're going to survive the evening even if something huge goes wrong. Any guest who's ever hosted a party will sympathize with you, and any guest who hasn't will probably still take pity on you (plus they'll be learning from your composed example)—as long as you don't turn into Evil Hostess.

Learn a lesson from Holly, who can best be described as being a meticulous person. Her house is carefully organized, her wardrobe is always coordinated right down to the smallest detail, and her parties are orchestrated to the second. Holly is wound a little tight, but she learned the importance of letting some things slide: "I used to be so horrible when I was hosting a party. I would bark orders, cringe when someone disturbed the centerpiece, and practically faint if something big went wrong. I *never* enjoyed my own parties. When it got to the point that I didn't want to have people in my house anymore, I had to take a good look at myself. You know, other people have parties and they don't break into a cold sweat if someone dribbles cocktail sauce on the tablecloth, like I used to.

"I had to relax *a lot* and realize that hosting a party doesn't mean that absolutely everything has to be perfect. No one ever expected perfection except me. I still have a higher standard for a successful party than most people do, I think, but I can handle it now when someone breaks a glass, or if the broccoli I've set out smells funny."

This is good advice from a (somewhat) reformed control freak. Stinky crudités will not ruin the entire evening.

Averting Disaster

So, what about your party? How did everything work out? Did the stripper show up on time and in the right costume? Did the caterer deliver the menu items you ordered for a sit-down dinner? Did the limo pick up you and the girls at the correct time?

If something went wrong with the services you hired, was it because you didn't remember to call and confirm your order? While many hostesses overlook this step once they've signed a contract, the best way to make sure you're going to get what you've paid for is to call in advance to confirm it.

 FACT

It's like the old saying goes, "The squeaky wheel gets the grease." The hostess who gets on the horn and makes a company read their copy of the contract to her is more likely to be satisfied with the service.

Jeannie is a big advocate of confirming services ever since she averted a near-disaster while she was planning a bachelorette party for her best friend. "I called the hotel where we had booked some rooms to make absolutely sure that we had a block of rooms—we obviously didn't want to be scattered from end to end of this huge hotel.

"When I called, the girl at the desk told me that although our rooms were booked, they weren't in a block—they *were* all over the place. Since I had called two weeks in advance, she was able to move us around so that we were all on the same floor, at least, but we would have been furious if we had checked in and found out we weren't even staying in the same wing.

Someone in the hotel made an error when they booked separate rooms all over the place for us, *but* it was easily fixed by making one phone call."

Guests—Who Needs Them?

With a little planning and a little luck, it's likely that any party will get off to a good start. However, a party's success also depends on the guests. It's not always someone's fault—sometimes the guest list is just a bad mix of people. Unfortunately, if you're planning a bachelorette party, putting together the guest list isn't always up to you. Often, certain friends and family have to be included in some pre-wedding events. Sometimes, it's not even up to the bride to decide on who gets excluded in her bachelorette bash.

 QUESTION?

If a few of the guests were critical of my bachelorette party, was my party was a failure?
It's not pleasant to hear people criticize the project to which you had devoted so much of your time. But you need to be prepared for this kind of response. If the majority of the guests had a good time and complimented you on doing a great job, don't take the complaints of the surly minority to heart—it's impossible to please all of the people all of the time anyway.

But if you've managed to have a fun party even with the bride's future sister-in-law trying to dampen everyone's moods, it's probably because you've figured out the secret of dealing with party guests—while you can't always control your guests, you can control your party. Sometimes simple actions like moving the party to a new locale will help diffuse tension that could potentially result in a blowup and an early end to your party.

 ## Dealing with Difficult Guests

Don't let one bad experience with the wrong combination of personalities scare you away from hosting another party. The following quiz represents some common guest pitfalls—do you recognize your party in these scenarios?

1. Your friend Madge insisted on bringing a plate of pastries even though you told her the caterer was providing dessert. You honestly didn't want homemade, bake-sale type sweets on the table. Were you right to be annoyed with her?

    a. Yes, and you should have chucked those cookies in the trash to make your point.
    b. Only if the sweets didn't taste all that great.
    c. No, she was just being nice.

The answer should be clear—you had no right to be annoyed, and she was just being nice.

Remember that guests who feel compelled to bring something to a party are following a general rule of etiquette that states that one should never show up empty-handed. She was trying to be helpful, so you should forgive this transgression.

2. The bride's coworker thought the stripper looked good enough to taste—literally. This behavior disturbed you so much, you were tempted to ask her to stop. What would have been the right thing to do?

   a. Keeping quiet—asking the guest to stop would be going too far.
   b. Asking the guest to stop.
   c. Telling the stripper he's all set and may now leave.

   Although you may be tempted to avoid a confrontation by asking the stripper to leave early, it's really not fair to the other guests, and you're perfectly justified in asking the crazy guest to stop and even leave the party. After all, you hired the stripper to dance—being licked by bachelorette party guests probably wasn't in the contract. As the hostess, you have every right to stop this kind of behavior.

3. The bride's mom was invited to the bachelorette party. She complained from the time she arrived to

the time she (thankfully) left. Nothing was right. The food was horrible, the other guests were stupid, and the gifts were horrifying. How could this have been handled?

  a. By throwing her out on her ear.
  b. By asking her to close her trap.
  c. By having a chat with the bride before you sent out invitations.

The answer is c. Next time you offer to throw a bachelorette party that will include the bride's mom, have a talk with the bride beforehand—make sure that the mom will want to be included. Inviting her mom will make the mother feel obligated, and if she doesn't want to be there, she's going to make your night a living hell.

4. Everyone else had a great time, but the bride spent the night throwing tantrums. She wanted the stripper to be dressed as a cowboy, not a fireman; she wanted a piñata; and she wanted real gifts. What was her problem?

  a. A delayed case of bratty adolescence.
  b. PMS.
  c. You two had very different ideas about this party.

Although it's possible that immaturity or PMS was to blame, the likeliest answer is that you and the bride had a communication problem. You were kind enough to host a bachelorette party for her, but she was expecting a completely different kind of evening. It's no excuse for her behavior, of course, but the next time you host a bachelorette party, you may want to have a long talk with the bride in the planning stages.

5. One of your guests got so wickedly drunk that she was harassing the other guests. Because she wouldn't stop even after you asked her to, you sent her home with another guest early on in the evening. Now, the guests are saying you stepped out of bounds and should apologize. What do you think?

    a. Ignore the problem. *You* are the one owed an apology from the guest for almost ruining a party you worked so hard to plan.
    a. Talk to the bride and see if she can calm the tension among her friends.
    a. Reconsider your decision and apologize to the guest for sending her home.

    You're certainly not obligated to do anything. You were the boss of the evening. You were protecting your guests from a belligerent, unpleasant attendee. You were well within your rights to dispose of her. She owes you an apology, not the other way around. However, if you do want to smooth things out and not cause any trouble for the bride, you may want to talk to her and see what she can do.

6. Talk about tension! Your guests did not get along with one another at all. You think you have failed your introductory course in hosting a party. What could you have done differently?

   a. Played more party games.
   b. Provided more opportunity for dancing.
   c. Sadly, nothing.

   Sometimes, despite your best efforts, your guests won't mingle well. Because they often bring very different families and friends together, wedding parties are brimming with this potential for trouble. There's very little you can do if separate groups decided to shut each other out. You did your best. Keep these groups in separate arenas from now on.

7. You hired a stripper, purchased sex toys and sexually themed party favors, and were ready to have a good time, but your guests seemed to be uncomfortable with all of that. What should you have done?

   a. Pressured them to participate—once they were more comfortable, they would have thanked you.
   b. Told them, "This is the theme of this party. Like it or lump it."

c. Offered to take down every offensive decoration and make it a clean party.

The answer is b. Lay down the law, but don't force anyone into anything. Bachelorette parties have a reputation for being risqué and naughty, so the majority of guests will arrive expecting to see racy decorations or a stripper. Guests who object to this should be told, in no uncertain terms, that you won't be undecorating the living room, nor will the stripper be turned away at the door. You have put the ball in their court; they can leave if they're uncomfortable.

8. Men came crashing through your front door! The groom and his pals were the uninvited guests who showed up and stuffed the stripper into his car. Then, they proceeded to eat all of your food, drink all of your alcohol, and generally ruin the girls-only feel of the night. Whose responsibility was it to make them leave?

   a. Every guest should have banded together to fight the intruders.
   b. It was your responsibility as hostess.
   c. The bride's marrying this clown—she should have handled it.

   Both b and c are correct. The bride is the one who is going to have the most leverage with the groom and his cronies. A stern word from her will often take care of gatecrashers. But since it's your house and your party, you have every right in the world to ask uninvited guests to leave.

 QUESTION?

So, how did you do?
Even if you didn't pass the test with flying colors, now you know a little more about crowd control and will be able to handle your guests a little more sternly—if need be—the next time around.

Surviving a Flop

If your reaction now is, "Oh! I could have done that and things would have been better!" don't beat yourself up. The majority of hostesses have survived at least one flop of a party that haunts them. Any hostess who tells you she has never had a bad party either hasn't had all that many or has a short and selective memory.

It's not necessarily the worst thing in the world to have a flop under your belt. There's really no better way to learn the right way to do things than to experience firsthand the wrong way to do them. This section covers some common misconceptions (read: excuses) that depressed hostesses give for their bad parties.

I'm Not a Planner

This is a pretty good excuse, but it's not going to fly. In order to survive in this world, you *have* to plan things, even if it's on the most basic level. You need clothes, don't you? You eat, right? If you have a car, you must keep track of when you're low on gas or when to get the next oil change. These are things you plan— you're going to buy new shoes on Tuesday right after work; you're going to go to the grocery store and get everything you need for tomato soup and grilled cheese; you really need to stop at the gas station or you'll be pushing that car home.

Ratchet that planning up a level to the next step. You schedule your hair appointments and doctor appointments, and you keep track of your checking account so that every other check you write doesn't bounce, sending you to bad-credit hell. This is also basic planning.

Now, if you're a mature adult making things work day-to-day (you show up for work, you're dressed and fed, and you know where your checkbook is), you are a planner. You can absolutely handle the basics of planning a party. You just need to look at it a little differently.

If, for example, you felt overwhelmed by taking on everything all at once, pace yourself next time. Start early enough so that you won't have to call the entertainment agency to interview a stripper, the limo company, and the caterer all in one day.

ESSENTIAL

> Spreading the planning tasks out over time will really ease you into the party. As long as you keep yourself organized, you'll be chipping away at the mountain of planning more than you realize—and you'll be finished before you realize how much work you've accomplished.

I'm Just So Disorganized

People who plead disorganization are usually keeping a secret: They *like* being disorganized. To them, disorganization is order. There's nothing wrong with that, actually, as long as it works for you and isn't causing any major upheavals in your life. Walk into any disorganized person's home and chances are she knows right where everything is—or can at least get pretty close to what she's looking for.

Unfortunately, planning a party does require you to become organized on a more universal level. You can't have contracts on the coffee table, receipts in your junk drawer, and the guest list under the couch and expect your next party to go off without a hitch.

Again, move to the most basic level of organization next time. If you hate the idea of having a separate file or folder for each category of your planning, then at least get one folder and put everything in there. This would send a truly organized person into a tailspin, but for a clutter-lover, this is the easiest way to keep all of your important documents together.

So the next time you host a bachelorette party, you'll know whether or not you ever invited the bride's cousin, who was conspicuously absent from the party you just hosted, and later claimed she never got an invitation. (You know you meant to send her one, but did you or not? You did. Or didn't you? You did. You think.)

 ALERT!

A spending hangover is actually a good lesson in disguise. Now you know you don't need to go completely overboard to make a friend happy—and you should *never* host a lavish party with the expectation that your friend will do the same thing for you when you're getting married. That's setting yourself up for a *huge* disappointment.

I Can't Afford Another Party—*Ever*

If you *way* overspent on this bachelorette party with the intention of giving your engaged friend the biggest and best sendoff anyone has ever seen (the fireworks were an especially nice touch), you may be feeling that knot in the pit of your stomach tightening as you realize that you really didn't need to do all of that. Now, how are you going to pay off all those bills?

The next time you host a bachelorette party for

someone, draw up your budget early on and stick to it. You do not need to have the very best of everything, as you probably realize now. The cheaper wine would have been fine; one stripper would have been all right—you didn't need three of them; and you could have played recorded music instead of hiring a live band.

 ESSENTIAL

In the event that you feel you absolutely must host another spectacular and incredibly expensive party, don't do it alone. Get a cohost or two to help out with the planning and the cost. That way you can still do things on a larger scale, and you won't be sleeping on a park bench because you used your rent money to get the *jumbo* shrimp.

The Wedding's Off—And It's My Fault!

If the bride did something so distasteful and unacceptable at her bachelorette party that her fiancé broke off the engagement, this is *not* your fault, unless you had a direct and premeditated hand in whatever it is she did. (The two of you decided that selling narcotics—instead of candies from a necklace—would be a good idea, and then the bride got arrested and missed her wedding. Yeah, that's partially your fault.)

If she went and kissed some other man, you really can't take the blame for that, even though others may try to pin some of it on you. The bride is presumably a big girl who is responsible for her own actions. Unless you stood there cheering her on and lining up men for her to make out with, she stands alone on this one. Anyone who tries to make you feel bad for taking her out for her bachelorette party is wrong. It's that simple.

What a Letdown

So, nothing went terribly wrong. The guests behaved themselves admirably, you aren't broke, and the bride and groom are still together, as in love as ever. But something feels funny. A common postparty complaint for anyone—hostesses, guests of honor, and guests alike—is that the party wasn't as good as you thought it was going to be, and for no particular reason. The food was good, the music was fine, the gifts were extremely amusing, so why are you blue?

Having a party end is either a blessing or a curse. If you were dreading it and things went off more smoothly than you ever could have imagined, then you're probably looking forward to your next event, whatever that may be. But if you spent the months of planning looking forward to this awesome night as most bachelorette hostesses do, then it's absolutely normal to feel a little sad when everything's over. It has less to do with being a hostess and more to do with being a human being. Everyone feels this way after a fun time ends. It's like Christmas—you look forward to it, you count the days, you're bursting with excitement and singing carols, and then suddenly, it's December 26 and what the heck are you supposed to do now?

Of course, that may be part of the reason you're feeling down. This was your last official "hurrah" with your soon-to-be-married friend, and maybe you're afraid that things are going to change drastically once she puts that wedding band on. Unfortunately, there's no way to predict the future of your relationship with the bride-to-be, and worrying about it often only fuels your worst fears—things that will most likely not happen.

 ALERT!

> Don't take one rejection as a slap in the face. The same emotions that were running high before the wedding have now morphed into post-wedding confusion. You girls may need to have a heart-to-heart chat and lay it on the table. You don't want to be shot down every time you ask her to join you, but she doesn't want to go out drinking anymore. Meet in the middle.

If you got stinking drunk and did some things you'd rather not remember—and you really wish everyone else would stop telling you the details—all you can do is drink some water, take some aspirin, and let time take its course. Next weekend someone else will be in the spotlight and you'll be off the hook. Here's another good lesson learned: Stop at fun-drunk before you move into stupid-drunk. You'll thank yourself in the morning.

Letting Go

Often, girlfriends of the bride are just as excited as she is about the upcoming wedding. It's easy to get swept up in all the hoopla and parties, even when you're not the guest of honor. When it's all over, the bride has a new life to settle into and you have . . . the same life you had before. Except you think you've lost your newly married friend for good.

A bride's got to do what a bride's got to do—and she *has* to choose her new husband over her friends. At least, she should. Otherwise, there's no point to making the relationship a legal one. But don't despair. She's not gone forever. Here are some ways to keep your friendship alive after the parties end.

Keep In Touch

It sounds silly and almost moronically simple, but it's surprising how many single girls cut their married friends out of their lives—and vice versa—because of misconceptions. Single girls who either feel that the bride wants nothing to do with them or who feel that the bride thinks she's in a better place don't want to handle the rejection of having their married friend say, "Sorry, I've got to rub my hubby's feet tonight."

Likewise, once a girl ties the knot, she may feel funny about asking her single friends to meet somewhere other than their usual hotspots—she doesn't want to spoil their fun, but she doesn't want to go out club-hopping, either. If the bride is the first of your group of friends to get married, she may not know how to handle her new position of being the only one with a husband.

Give her a call. Ask her to go to out for dinner. Don't count her out just because she's married. She may be agonizing over how to approach the rest of you girls.

Keep Assumptions to a Minimum

Don't conclude that the bride is so blinded by her new domestic situation that she's forgotten all about you. If you've called her and she can't make it to meet you girls this weekend, it may be that she's busy with work, or she has to see her in-laws, or she just has other plans.

Nadia made that mistake when her friend Ellie got married. "I was just so mad that she always chose her husband over us—the friends she'd had since high school," Nadia says. "I had a huge birthday party for one of our other friends, and Ellie couldn't come because she had to go to a baptism for her husband's nephew or something like that. Nine out of ten times, she couldn't make it to whatever we were doing. It just got to the point where we stopped asking her to do things with us."

So what do you think happened? Ellie read those signs loud and clear, and stopped calling her old friends, who, in her opinion, were being "childish and spiteful." Ellie explains her side of the story: "They could never accept that I had things I had to do. When I got married, I automatically got another family in the deal—my husband's. Maybe I *would* rather go to a friend's birthday party than to a communion, but that choice is pretty much out of my hands, unless I want my husband to blow off my family's big functions for things he'd rather be doing.

 FACT

> If things seem good between the two of you otherwise, you may just have to accept that her life *has* changed. She will have obligations now that she didn't have before. Ending your friendship because she doesn't have the same amount of free time she had before is something you'll regret later.

"My old friends all started making comments about how they never thought they'd see me being pushed around by a man, and that's not how it was at all. I was the only married one in the group, and I just got sick of the whole thing, especially when I had other, married friends who understood when my husband and I couldn't make it to their barbecues because we had other things to do.

"I wasn't about to justify my relationship with my

husband to my old friends, so I dropped out of sight. By my first anniversary, I wasn't speaking to many them anymore. Could I have balanced my husband and my friends? I think so, if my friends hadn't been so quick to judge."

Now that Nadia is older and married, she acknowledges that she and her girlfriends were too hard on Ellie, but the damage was done way back when, and is beyond repair.

 ESSENTIAL

> Don't jump to conclusions. The bride and groom are definitely going to want their space at first, but they're not cutting out their friends forever. In fact, some newlyweds find their new situation a little stressful, but are reluctant to admit it to anyone. All of the sudden, your friend has become a wife. It can be an overwhelming feeling when she first realizes the significance of this word.

If the bride is acting strangely, give her time. She'll be back to her old self soon enough, once she determines who she is in her new marriage. And if you've been a nice, supportive friend in the meantime, instead of being judgmental and kind of mean to her, you'll pick up your friendship where you left off.

Keep Her in Mind

If all else fails and the bride really is the one acting like she can't associate with her old friends anymore, there's nothing to do but deal with it. Weddings can do strange things to people's heads—some women think they can only have married friends or they have to behave a certain way now that they're carrying the title "Mrs."

The good news is that this is usually a temporary side effect of the bride having steeped herself in all things matrimonial for the past year. She'll come around eventually and realize that the world did not, in fact, stop turning on the day she got married. Sometimes it takes another more recently married, self-involved bride to show her the error of her ways. (Seeing someone else mirror her own annoying behavior can be an alarming thing to a newlywed.)

Most women eventually realize that no one can ever take the place of an old friend. Until she comes around, keep her on the back burner of your mind, at least. You two have come this far together—give her a little time. She'll be back.

Appendix A
Planner's Checklist

It's been said time and time again—the most important part of hosting a party is to be prepared and plan in advance. Use the following checklist to keep track of what you need to accomplish as the party draws nearer.

Six months to a year in advance

◯ Discuss the party idea with the bride-to-be.

◯ Start putting together the guest list.

◯ If the bachelorette party will be held in the spring or early summer (wedding and prom season), start calling around and booking limos, restaurants, caterers, hotel rooms—any service you'll be paying for.

Three months in advance

◯ Start thinking about your party theme and menu.

◯ Finalize booking all the services you will require (limo, restaurants, etc.).

◯ Book a stripper.

Two months in advance

◯ This is a good time to place your Internet orders for any decorations or gifts you will need for the party. (You need to be prepared in case shipping is slow or you need to exchange any of your orders.)

One month in advance

◯ It's time to finalize all your decisions—the theme, food, decorations, and entertainment.

◯ Now is when you should be sending out the invitations. (Make sure you send them all out at the same time, in one bundle.)

Two weeks in advance

◯ Make sure you call and confirm your arrangements for the limo, the caterer, the hotel rooms, the stripper, and so forth. Get confirmation numbers, if possible. Ask your last-minute questions.

The week of the party

◯ Start making final preparations. If you're cooking, buy your groceries and prepare the foods that can be stored in the freezer.

◯ Make sure to stock plenty of alcohol.

◯ Get your house cleaned and your decorations ready to go, wrap the door prizes, and plan the games.

The day before the party

At this point, you should be totally prepared. Go through your final checklist: Have the hired services been confirmed? Do you absolutely, positively know who's coming and who's not? Did you call the neighbors and let them know that loud music will be coming from your house? Is the bar stocked? Now relax, and have a good time!

Appendix B

A Quick Bartending Guide

In this appendix, you'll find some easy-to-make popular drinks that will be perfect for your guests. Some can be made with or without alcohol (as noted).

Everybody's Fave Punch

Makes approximately 35 servings

2 gallons fruit punch
2 (2-liter) bottles ginger ale
½ gallon sherbet
2½–3 cups (or to taste) vodka, if desired

1. Mix together the fruit punch and ginger ale in punch bowl.
2. Use a spoon to scoop thin ribbons of sherbet on top of the punch mixture.
3. If desired, add vodka to taste.

Ruby Red Wine Punch

Makes approximately 20 servings

1 bottle red wine	1 cup raspberry syrup
1 cup lemon juice	Ice
¾ cup granulated sugar	1 quart club soda

1. Combine all the ingredients *except* the ice and club soda. Stir until all the sugar is dissolved.
2. Pour into a punch bowl over ice; stir well.
3. Add the soda just before serving.

Wedding Belle Punch

Makes approximately 15 servings

¼ cup granulated sugar
10 ounces frozen strawberries, thawed
1 bottle champagne, chilled
1 bottle rosé wine

1. Place the sugar and strawberries (with their juices) in a punch bowl; stir to dissolve the sugar.
2. Add the champagne and wine. Serve chilled.

Sangria

Makes approximately 6 servings

1 bottle red wine (type of your preference)
2 ounces lime juice
4 ounces rum
Slices of peaches and other fruit

Mix together the wine, lime juice, and rum in a pitcher. Add the fruit slices. Serve in wineglasses.

Virgin Mary

Makes 1 drink

8 ounces tomato juice
1 teaspoon Worcestershire sauce
Dash horseradish
Dash ground black pepper
Dash hot sauce
A few ice cubes
Celery stalks

Mix together all the ingredients *except* the celery in a shaker, according to taste. Add the celery stalk as garnish.

Bloody Mary

Makes 1 drink

Virgin Mary (see previous recipe)
1½ ounces vodka

Prepare the Virgin Mary and add the vodka to the shaker; shake well. Serve in a chilled glass.

Lemon Daisy (nonalcoholic)

Makes 1 drink

2 ounces lemon juice (or juice of 1 lemon)
1 ounce grenadine (pomegranate syrup)
Ice
1 ounce lemon and lime soda
1 ounce sparkling water
Lemon slice

1. Pour the lemon juice and grenadine over the ice in an old-fashioned glass; stir well.
2. Add equal parts lemon and lime soda and sparkling water; stir gently. Add a lemon twist for garnish.

Margarita on the Rocks

Makes 1 drink

1½ ounces tequila	Ice
1 ounce lime juice	Salt
½ ounce Triple Sec	Lime wedge

1. Combine the tequila, lime juice, and Triple Sec in a shaker and fill the shaker halfway with ice; shake well.
2. Strain into a salt-rimmed margarita or cocktail glass. Garnish with a lime wedge.

Piña Colada

Makes 1 drink

2 ounces light rum	Ice
2 ounces coconut cream	Pineapple slice
4 ounces pineapple juice	Cherry

1. Combine the first 4 ingredients in a blender in the order they are listed; blend thoroughly.
2. Pour into a collins or parfait glass. Serve with a pineapple slice, a cherry, and a straw.

Coy Colada (nonalcoholic)

Makes 1 drink

2 ounces coconut cream
6 ounces pineapple juice
1 teaspoon lime juice
Ice
Pineapple slice
Cherry

1. Combine the first 4 ingredients in a blender in the order they are listed; blend thoroughly.
2. Pour into a collins or parfait glass. Serve with a pineapple slice, a cherry, and a straw.

Sour-Apple Martini

Makes 1 drink

1 ounce melon-flavored liqueur
2 ounces sour-apple-flavored liqueur
1 ounce vodka
Ice

1. Combine all the ingredients in a shaker, filling the shaker halfway with the ice; shake well.
2. Strain into a martini glass, and serve.

Cosmopolitan

Makes 1 drink

1 ounce citrus-flavored vodka
½ ounce Cointreau
½ ounce cranberry juice
¼ ounce lime juice
Ice

1. Combine the ingredients in a shaker, filling the shaker halfway with the ice; shake well.
2. Strain into a cocktail glass.

Jiggly-Wiggly Shots

Makes about 15 to 20 shots

1½ cup boiling water
1½ (¼-ounce) packages flavored gelatin
1 cup vodka

1. Combine the water and gelatin; stir until completely dissolved. Add the vodka and mix well.
2. Pour the mixture into 1-ounce plastic serving cups and place on a tray in the refrigerator. Serve chilled.

Blowjob Shot

Makes 1 shot

½ ounce vodka
½ ounce coffee brandy
½ ounce coffee liqueur
Ice
Whipped cream

1. Combine the ingredients in a shaker, filling the shaker halfway with the ice; shake well.
2. Strain into a shot glass. Squirt whipped cream on top.

Traditionally, the bride-to-be cannot use her hands while doing these shots.

Parisian Blonde Shooter

Makes 1 shot

½ ounce light rum
½ ounce Triple Sec
½ ounce dark rum
Ice

1. Combine the ingredients in a shaker, filling the shaker halfway with the ice; shake well.
2. Strain into a shot glass.

Appendix C

Additional Resources

There's a wealth of information and advice for the hostess who's curious to learn more. From Web sites listing perfect party recipes to books that guide you through guest etiquette, here's where you can turn if you need additional help.

Books

All About Party Food and Drinks, by Irma S. Rombauer, Marion Romabauer Becker, and Ethan Becker (New York: Scribner, 2002). From the creators of *The Joy of Cooking* comes a cookbook perfect for your party.

The Bartender's Bible: 1001 Mixed Drinks and Everything You Need to Know to Set Up Your Bar, by Gary Regan (New York: Harper Mass Market Paperbacks, 1993). Need a drink? This book offers more than 1,000 recipes, including nonalcoholic beverages. Also offered are tips on setting up your bar and serving your drinks properly.

Be My Guest: Theme Party Savoir-Faire, by Rena Kirdar Sindi and Jessica Craig-Martin (New York: Assouline Publishing, 2002). Covers everything you need to plan a spectacular theme party, whether it's a small occasion or a major affair.

Games People Play: The Biggest and Best Book of Party Games and Activities, by Penny Warner (Minnetonka, MN: Meadowbrook, 1998). There are loads of party games here. Take your pick and plan your party around a few of them!

Great Games for Great Parties: How to Throw a Perfect Party, by Andrea Campbell and Sanford Hoffman, illustrator (London: Sterling Publications, 1992). In this book, you'll find advice on getting the party rolling and keeping it moving in the right direction. Includes more than 100 party games.

Emily Post's Entertaining: A Classic Guide to Adding Elegance and Ease to Any Festive Occasion, by Peggy Post (New York: HarperPerennial, 1998). Etiquette and tips for any sort of party—large or small, formal or casual.

The $50 Dinner Party: 26 Dinner Parties That Won't Break Your Bank, Your Back or Your Schedule, by Sally Sampson (Columbus, OH: Fireside Books, 1998). This volume is perfect for the fearful first-time hostess. You'll get help on learning how to entertain on a budget and there are recipes diverse enough for every taste.

30 Minute Entertaining, by Louise Pickford (San Diego, CA: Laurel Glen, 2000). Get more information on how to host a party and enjoy it, too! Includes recipes for all kinds of gatherings.

Magazines

Bon Appétit. Get entertaining inspiration from this wonderfully put together magazine.

Cuisine at Home. Check it out for recipes with detailed how-to instructions. Includes a "Faster with Fewer" section, which focuses on recipes with five or less ingredients that can be prepared in fifteen minutes or less. Perfect for the nervous cook!

Playgirl. Need some quick decorations? Grab a copy of this magazine and get some scissors—and *voilà*! Instant party!

Web Sites

- *www.pamperedchef.com* This user-friendly Web site offers information on hosting parties and ordering kitchenware.

- *www.evites.com* Who needs the fuss of snail mail? This online invitation Web site will make your life *really* easy. Includes an RSVP chart to keep track of who's coming and who isn't.

- *www.customink.com* T-shirts, hats, and cups available to customize with your own racy messages.

- *www.bacheloretteparYfun.com* Everything you need but are too embarrassed to buy in person—adult gifts, risqué party favors, naughty decorations, and crazy games.

- *www.barmeister.com* Planning to have a wild drinking bash? This creative Web site has more drinking games than you could ever play in your life.

- *www.party411.com* Want more unique entertainment ideas, helpful tips, and party supplies? This Web site is your ticket to all that—it's a one-stop shopping and information center.

- *www.chocolatefantasies.com* Shockingly shaped candies, bachelorette party supplies, aromatherapy, Kama sutra, adult gifts, and games can all be purchased here.

- *www.webtender.com* Need a drink recipe? It's here! Thousands of drinks listed, along with a great search engine that makes finding a particular beverage a snap!

Index

We Have EVERYTHING!

BUSINESS

Everything® **Business Planning Book**
Everything® **Coaching and Mentoring Book**
Everything® **Fundraising Book**
Everything® **Home-Based Business Book**
Everything® **Leadership Book**
Everything® **Managing People Book**
Everything® **Network Marketing Book**
Everything® **Online Business Book**
Everything® **Project Management Book**
Everything® **Selling Book**
Everything® **Start Your Own Business Book**
Everything® **Time Management Book**

COMPUTERS

Everything® **Build Your Own Home Page Book**
Everything® **Computer Book**
Everything® **Internet Book**
Everything® **Microsoft® Word 2000 Book**

COOKBOOKS

Everything® **Barbecue Cookbook**
Everything® **Bartender's Book, $9.95**
Everything® **Chinese Cookbook**
Everything® **Chocolate Cookbook**
Everything® **Cookbook**
Everything® **Dessert Cookbook**
Everything® **Diabetes Cookbook**
Everything® **Low-Carb Cookbook**
Everything® **Low-Fat High-Flavor Cookbook**
Everything® **Mediterranean Cookbook**
Everything® **Mexican Cookbook**
Everything® **One-Pot Cookbook**
Everything® **Pasta Book**
Everything® **Quick Meals Cookbook**
Everything® **Slow Cooker Cookbook**
Everything® **Soup Cookbook**
Everything® **Thai Cookbook**
Everything® **Vegetarian Cookbook**
Everything® **Wine Book**

HEALTH

Everything® **Anti-Aging Book**
Everything® **Diabetes Book**
Everything® **Dieting Book**
Everything® **Herbal Remedies Book**
Everything® **Hypnosis Book**
Everything® **Menopause Book**
Everything® **Nutrition Book**
Everything® **Reflexology Book**
Everything® **Stress Management Book**
Everything® **Vitamins, Minerals, and Nutritional Supplements Book**

HISTORY

Everything® **American History Book**
Everything® **Civil War Book**
Everything® **Irish History & Heritage Book**
Everything® **Mafia Book**
Everything® **World War II Book**

HOBBIES & GAMES

Everything® **Bridge Book**
Everything® **Candlemaking Book**
Everything® **Casino Gambling Book**
Everything® **Chess Basics Book**
Everything® **Collectibles Book**
Everything® **Crossword and Puzzle Book**
Everything® **Digital Photography Book**
Everything® **Family Tree Book**
Everything® **Games Book**
Everything® **Knitting Book**
Everything® **Magic Book**
Everything® **Motorcycle Book**
Everything® **Online Genealogy Book**
Everything® **Photography Book**
Everything® **Pool & Billiards Book**
Everything® **Quilting Book**
Everything® **Scrapbooking Book**
Everything® **Soapmaking Book**

HOME IMPROVEMENT

Everything® **Feng Shui Book**
Everything® **Gardening Book**
Everything® **Home Decorating Book**
Everything® **Landscaping Book**
Everything® **Lawn Care Book**
Everything® **Organize Your Home Book**

KIDS' STORY BOOKS

Everything® **Bedtime Story Book**
Everything® **Bible Stories Book**
Everything® **Fairy Tales Book**
Everything® **Mother Goose Book**

LANGUAGE

Everything® **Learning French Book**

Everything® **Learning German Book**

Everything® **Learning Italian Book**

Everything® **Learning Latin Book**

Everything® **Learning Spanish Book**

Everything® **Sign Language Book**

MUSIC

Everything® **Drums Book (with CD), $19.95 ($31.95 CAN)**

Everything® **Guitar Book**

Everything® **Playing Piano and Keyboards Book**

Everything® **Rock & Blues Guitar Book (with CD), $19.95 ($31.95 CAN)**

Everything® **Songwriting Book**

NEW AGE

Everything® **Astrology Book**

Everything® **Divining the Future Book**

Everything® **Dreams Book**

Everything® **Ghost Book**

Everything® **Meditation Book**

Everything® **Numerology Book**

Everything® **Palmistry Book**

Everything® **Psychic Book**

Everything® **Spells & Charms Book**

Everything® **Tarot Book**

Everything® **Wicca and Witchcraft Book**

PARENTING

Everything® **Baby Names Book**

Everything® **Baby Shower Book**

Everything® **Baby's First Food Book**

Everything® **Baby's First Year Book**

Everything® **Breastfeeding Book**

Everything® **Father-to-Be Book**

Everything® **Get Ready for Baby Book**

Everything® **Home-schooling Book**

Everything® **Parent's Guide to Positive Discipline**

Everything® **Potty Training Book, $9.95 ($15.95 CAN)**

Everything® **Pregnancy Book, 2nd Ed.**

Everything® **Pregnancy Fitness Book**

Everything® **Pregnancy Organizer, $15.00 ($22.95 CAN)**

Everything® **Toddler Book**

Everything® **Tween Book**

PERSONAL FINANCE

Everything® **Budgeting Book**

Everything® **Get Out of Debt Book**

Everything® **Get Rich Book**

Everything® **Homebuying Book, 2nd Ed.**

Everything® **Homeselling Book**

Everything® **Investing Book**

Everything® **Money Book**

Everything® **Mutual Funds Book**

Everything® **Online Investing Book**

Everything® **Personal Finance Book**

Everything® **Personal Finance in Your 20s & 30s Book**

Everything® **Wills & Estate Planning Book**

PETS

Everything® **Cat Book**

Everything® **Dog Book**

Everything® **Dog Training and Tricks Book**

Everything® **Horse Book**

Everything® **Puppy Book**

Everything® **Tropical Fish Book**

REFERENCE

Everything® **Astronomy Book**

Everything® **Car Care Book**

Everything® **Christmas Book, $15.00 ($21.95 CAN)**

Everything® **Classical Mythology Book**

Everything® **Einstein Book**

Everything® **Etiquette Book**

Everything® **Great Thinkers Book**

Everything® **Philosophy Book**

Everything® **Shakespeare Book**

Everything® **Tall Tales, Legends, & Other Outrageous Lies Book**

Everything® **Toasts Book**

Everything® **Trivia Book**

Everything® **Weather Book**

RELIGION

Everything® **Angels Book**

Everything® **Buddhism Book**

Everything® **Catholicism Book**

Everything® **Jewish History & Heritage Book**

Everything® **Judaism Book**

Everything® **Prayer Book**

Everything® **Saints Book**

Everything® **Understanding Islam Book**

Everything® **World's Religions Book**

Everything® **Zen Book**

SCHOOL & CAREERS

Everything® **After College Book**

Everything® **College Survival Book**

Everything® **Cover Letter Book**

Everything® **Get-a-Job Book**

Everything® **Hot Careers Book**

Everything® **Job Interview Book**

Everything® **Online Job Search Book**

Everything® **Resume Book, 2nd Ed.**

Everything® **Study Book**

SELF-HELP

Everything® **Dating Book**
Everything® **Divorce Book**
Everything® **Great Marriage Book**
Everything® **Great Sex Book**
Everything® **Romance Book**
Everything® **Self-Esteem Book**
Everything® **Success Book**

SPORTS & FITNESS

Everything® **Bicycle Book**
Everything® **Body Shaping Book**
Everything® **Fishing Book**
Everything® **Fly-Fishing Book**
Everything® **Golf Book**
Everything® **Golf Instruction Book**
Everything® **Pilates Book**
Everything® **Running Book**
Everything® **Sailing Book, 2nd Ed.**
Everything® **T'ai Chi and QiGong Book**
Everything® **Total Fitness Book**
Everything® **Weight Training Book**
Everything® **Yoga Book**

TRAVEL

Everything® **Guide to Las Vegas**
Everything® **Guide to New England**
Everything® **Guide to New York City**
Everything® **Guide to Washington D.C.**
Everything® **Travel Guide to The Disneyland Resort®, California Adventure®, Universal Studios®, and the Anaheim Area**
Everything® **Travel Guide to the Walt Disney World Resort®, Universal Studios®, and Greater Orlando, 3rd Ed.**

WEDDINGS

Everything® **Bachelorette Party Book**
Everything® **Bridesmaid Book**
Everything® **Creative Wedding Ideas Book**
Everything® **Jewish Wedding Book**
Everything® **Wedding Book, 2nd Ed.**
Everything® **Wedding Checklist, $7.95 ($11.95 CAN)**
Everything® **Wedding Etiquette Book, $7.95 ($11.95 CAN)**
Everything® **Wedding Organizer, $15.00 ($22.95 CAN)**
Everything® **Wedding Shower Book, $7.95 ($12.95 CAN)**
Everything® **Wedding Vows Book, $7.95 ($11.95 CAN)**
Everything® **Weddings on a Budget Book, $9.95 ($15.95 CAN)**

WRITING

Everything® **Creative Writing Book**
Everything® **Get Published Book**
Everything® **Grammar and Style Book**
Everything® **Grant Writing Book**
Everything® **Guide to Writing Children's Books**
Everything® **Screenwriting Book**
Everything® **Writing Well Book**

EVERYTHING® KIDS' BOOKS

All titles are $6.95 and $10.95 CAN (unless otherwise noted)

Everything® **Kids' Baseball Book, 2nd Ed.**
Everything® **Kids' Bugs Book**
Everything® **Kids' Christmas Puzzle & Activity Book**
Everything® **Kids' Cookbook**
Everything® **Kids' Halloween Puzzle & Activity Book**
Everything® **Kids' Joke Book**
Everything® **Kids' Math Puzzles Book**
Everything® **Kids' Mazes Book**
Everything® **Kids' Money Book ($11.95 CAN)**
Everything® **Kids' Monsters Book**
Everything® **Kids' Nature Book ($11.95 CAN)**
Everything® **Kids' Puzzle Book**
Everything® **Kids' Science Experiments Book**
Everything® **Kids' Soccer Book**
Everything® **Kids' Travel Activity Book**